Formative
Language Assessment
for **English Learners**

Formative Language Assessment for **English Learners**

A Four-Step Process

Rita MacDonald
Timothy Boals
Mariana Castro
H. Gary Cook
Todd Lundberg
Paula A. White

HEINEMANN
Portsmouth, NH

Heinemann
361 Hanover Street
Portsmouth, NH 03801–3912
www.heinemann.com

Offices and agents throughout the world

The authors and publisher wish to thank those who have generously given permission to reprint borrowed material:

Excerpts from Common Core State Standards © Copyright 2010. National Governors Association Center for Best Practices and Council of Chief State School Officers. All rights reserved.

Cataloging-in-Publication Data is on file with the Library of Congress.
ISBN: 978-0-325-05357-8

Acquiring Editors: Yvonne S. and David E. Freeman
Editor: Holly Kim Price
Production Editor: Sonja S. Chapman
Typesetter: Valerie Levy, Drawing Board Studios
Cover and interior design: Suzanne Heiser
Manufacturing: Steve Bernier

Printed in the United States of America on acid-free paper
19 18 17 16 15 EBM 1 2 3 4 5

This book is
dedicated to the teachers
and students who helped with
this research, and to all educators
working toward educational
equity and success for
English learners.

CONTENTS

Acknowledgments   ix

Introduction Formative Assessment: Assessment for Learning   xi
   What Is Language Assessment for Formative Purposes?   xiv
   How Does Language Assessment for Formative Purposes Fit into Teaching and Learning?   xv
   The Process   xvii
   How We Have Structured This Book   xxi

CHAPTER 1   Teaching and Sampling Academic Language: Weaving a Language Focus into Content Lessons   1
   Academic Language   2
   Weaving Academic Language Instruction into Lessons   2
   Putting the Tools to Work: Clarifying Genre Expectations   5
   Final Thoughts: Gathering Samples of Students' Language   17

CHAPTER 2   Where Are We and Where Are We Going? Analyzing the Data and Identifying Language Learning Targets   18
   Four Lenses for Language Analysis   19
   Analyzing Language   22
   Writing Samples, Analyses, and Identification of LLTs   26
   Final Thoughts: Using Four Lenses to Set LLTs   37

CHAPTER 3   Involving Our Students in the Journey: Providing Formative Feedback   40
   What Does Effective Formative Feedback Look Like?   41
   Sources of Formative Feedback   42
   Providing Formative Feedback to Jorge, Kia, and Migdalia   43
   Final Thoughts: Using Effective Formative Feedback   52

CHAPTER 4   Staying on Course: Developing Tools to Gather Information About Student Progress   55
   Building Tools to Assess Language for Formative Purposes   56
   Creating Tools for the Three Students   60
   Final Thoughts: Building a Repertoire of Tools to Assess Language for Formative Purposes   69

CHAPTER 5   The Formative Assessment Cycle in Practice   70
   Implementing a Language-focused Formative Assessment Model   70
   Changing Ideas and Changing Practice   72
   Final Thoughts: Putting It All Together and Getting Back to the Students   73

Appendix
   About FLARE: Formative Language Assessment Records for English Language Learners   75
Glossary   78
References   81
Index   85

ACKNOWLEDGMENTS

The authors would like to extend their appreciation to the Carnegie Corporation of New York for its generous support of the Formative Language Assessment Records for English Language Learners (FLARE) project and to the three FLARE partner districts: Charlotte-Mecklenburg Schools, North Carolina; Chicago Public Schools, Illinois; and Garden Grove Unified School District, California. The authors would also like to thank the many individuals who have contributed their comments to earlier drafts, including Jennifer Daniels from WIDA, who provided a teacher's perspective of the manuscript. We would like to give a special thanks to Margaret Heritage and Ed Roeber, whose expertise and experience in formative assessment has guided this work and whose thoughtful feedback on an early draft clarified both our ideas and their expression.

Introduction

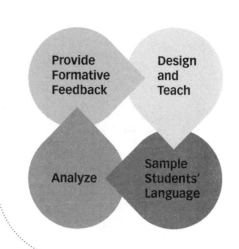

Formative Assessment: Assessment for Learning

"To many of today's teachers, assessment is synonymous with high-stakes standardized tests. But there is an entirely different kind of assessment that can actually transform teaching and learning."
—Margaret Heritage
(2007, p. 140)

High-stakes educational assessment is on all educators' minds these days. As local and state education agencies discuss how best to assess students' progress toward new educational goals, and evaluation of teacher performance is more and more frequently tied to student progress, these tests are shaping the educational landscape. Regardless of the effects of these tests and debates, teachers continue to sit next to students in classrooms across the country, doing their best to help students grasp the next important idea that they need to weave together a web of knowledge and skills to sustain them in their education, their careers, and their lives as citizens—and they are doing this for all students, including the increasing numbers of English Language Learners (ELLs) in their classrooms. High-stakes tests will have little to offer students and teachers as they discern the next steps, but there is a type of assessment that will make a difference.

This "different type of assessment" that Margaret Heritage refers to is *formative assessment*, which occurs in the midst of instruction and compares students' ongoing progress to possible trajectories of learning. It can help identify the most productive next steps in instruction. Excellent work on formative assessment (CCSSO 2012; Heritage 2007, 2010, 2013;

Assessments for Formative Purposes can include . . .					Formative Assessment means specifically . . .
1 year ago	I	I	I	X	TODAY
Interim assessments, given over several months to determine student progress over several units, are used to inform curriculum revision.					A teacher observes a student during a lesson and responds immediately with comments or questions to guide the student's attention or effort.

Figure I.1 The current formative assessment landscape

National Research Council 2001; Popham, 1995, 2008; Shute 2008; Wiliam 2012) has helped educators learn about and integrate this powerful tool into their repertoires. As educators explore the exciting possibilities presented by formative assessment, more nuanced understandings evolve. Today, the term *formative assessment* can mean different things depending on who is speaking, and some clarity regarding the terminology can be helpful.

If we envision formative assessment as the continuum shown in Figure I.1, we see that the specific term *formative assessment* has come to mean assessment that is literally in the moment: The teacher interacts in the moment with comments or questions to guide a student's attention or effort. The teacher does not go away to analyze student work against some criteria; her understanding of the learning trajectory and of the success criteria based on that trajectory is immediately available to her, as is her knowledge of multiple resources to support students' learning in the moment. This level of skill with immediate formative assessment and interaction is built up over time through solid training, support, and experience.

In contrast to this specific term, *assessment for formative purposes* is a much broader category of tools and processes that could be used to shape instruction over time. Some experts on formative assessment suggest that any type of assessment—even an annual test given to evaluate a program—can be considered "formative" if its results are used to analyze and shape instructional practices. In other words, the purpose for which assessment results are used, rather than their contingency to classroom instruction, is what categorizes an assessment as having a formative purpose. A major difference between these two types of assessment is the direct interaction with students as they are learning: Formative assessment involves ongoing interaction with students. Assessment for formative purposes may or may not.

The process we describe in this book falls at the X point on this continuum. We will be describing a process developed over five years of interaction with middle and high school teachers who wanted to learn how to better support students' language development during their instruction. With these teachers, we gathered frequent samples of student writing to analyze the language used and think about how best to support the next steps in students' language development. The analysis of student writing is rarely an "in the moment" interaction; therefore, the process we describe falls into the area of "assessment for formative purposes." The process we describe is very close to that instructional moment though. Student language is sampled during the course of an ongoing series of related lessons, when students are in the process of learning to write specific types of genres and when rewrites are expected as students are supported in their movement toward successful writing. Our process is situated well before the point at which student work is graded (a summative activity). The results are used to guide the upcoming teaching-learning interaction, by helping teachers shape the next steps in their instruction and assisting students in identifying the next steps in their learning—not "in the moment," but perhaps "in the upcoming moment." It may be that when teachers and students are familiar with using this process, they may use "in the moment" formative assessment.

This book offers an understanding of a process (not a test) that can be used by teachers and students to reflect on the effectiveness of students' language and to interact in productive ways to strengthen students' ability to use language effectively—all of it deeply contextualized and part of the ongoing flow of teaching and learning, not an "add-on." Because we have written from our experience, we focus on students' writing, a language domain that lends itself more easily to observation than do the receptive language domains of reading or listening, and one that results in a more easily studied artifact than does the other productive domain (speaking). The process we describe can serve as a foundation to reflect on and interact productively around student language in all language domains.

Few resources currently exist to assist educators in the use of formative assessment practices and strategies related to students' growing knowledge and skill with English, the medium through which teachers and learners convey ideas in most U.S. classrooms. Research currently underway on the Dynamic Language Learning Progression (www.dllp.org/) promises to provide detailed, empirically derived information about how language development progresses during the elementary school years, for both English learners and English-fluent students. At the secondary level, the Carnegie-funded Formative Language Assessment Records for English Language Learners (FLARE) project developed a process of language assessment that could be used for formative purposes with English Language Learners at the secondary level.

This book shares what we have learned about language assessment strategies for formative purposes for and with ELLs. This book grew out of five years of working with ELLs and their teachers through the FLARE project, where we collaborated with middle school and high school teachers in three school districts (Chicago Public Schools, Illinois; Charlotte-Mecklenburg Public Schools, North Carolina; and Garden Grove Unified School District, California) to develop language assessment practices that could be used formatively for ELLs in secondary classrooms. The project brought together research on learning progressions with the procedures, tools, and insights of the many teachers with whom we worked. What emerged from that project was a language-focused model for assessing language for formative purposes. This book presents the distillation of those five years of work: a series of steps for (a) weaving a language focus into content lessons, (b) sampling students' language, (c) analyzing students' language to help them broaden their linguistic choices and share ideas more effectively, and (d) creating and maintaining active partnerships with students as they learn and practice new ways to use English.

Each chapter in this book presents detailed information about the steps in the model. We illustrate each step of the process with examples. Although we present those steps separately, we want to stress that they often occur simultaneously and are woven into the fabric of teaching and learning.

This introduction provides background information about the process of assessing language for formative purposes, and it introduces the three teachers and three students whose stories we use to illustrate that process in the coming chapters.

What Is Language Assessment for Formative Purposes?

Language assessment for formative purposes is a systematic process of language analysis that provides students and teachers with feedback on students' progress toward specific instructional goals for using English. ELLs—the many students in American schools who are learning English as an additional language while they learn mathematics and science and social studies—are held to the same accountability standards as their English-proficient peers. Given that ELLs must simultaneously learn new content and a new language, they have been described as having to do "double the work" (Short & Fitzsimmons 2007). To succeed in this challenge, ELLs and their teachers need explicit information about their progress in acquiring knowledge, skills, and *academic language*. When teachers have the tools and knowledge needed to analyze student language and identify probable language learning trajectories and next steps, teachers can adjust their instruction accordingly to help students understand and engage actively in their own language development.

The work of clarifying learning goals is not limited to ELLs, of course. In *How People Learn*, Bransford, Brown, and Cocking (2000) pointed out that all students need ongoing information about their own progress and learning. In this book, and especially in this chapter, we explore the kind of information about progress and learning that ELLs need and describe a framework for gathering samples of students' language, analyzing those samples, and providing timely and actionable information, or *formative feedback*, to students to improve their learning. Formative feedback is information communicated to learners to improve learning (Shute 2008). By extension, formative *language* feedback is information communicated to learners to support their development of academic language.

Teachers have always worked to provide students with ongoing feedback on their progress, but this information has not always been specific enough to help students take the next, most attainable step in their academic language development. We've discovered in our work with teachers that they are interested in exploring ways to gather, analyze, and share specific information about language development with ELLs. Together with teachers, we've developed a process and tools to accomplish these goals. Teachers suggest that effective use of the process helps them gather the type of data they need to adjust ongoing instruction and to deliver the specific, actionable feedback ELLs need to improve their achievement of intended instructional and linguistic outcomes. Classrooms defined by effective assessment for language for formative purposes become dynamic spaces in which teachers and students alike develop deeper understandings of language and then use that information to plan clear, attainable steps to increase their effectiveness in communicating ideas in English.

How Does Language Assessment for Formative Purposes Fit into Teaching and Learning?

Teachers constantly observe student behavior to notice specific ways students respond to a task or activity and then make inferences about what their students are learning and the challenges they are facing. These inferences help teachers adjust curriculum, instruction, and assessment in their classrooms. Many teachers test their students in multiple ways to obtain information about conceptual or language development, but it is often too much of the wrong kind of assessment and too little of the right kind. To obtain a full and useful picture of students' progress in language learning, teachers need to work together with school leaders, students, and researchers to create a *balanced language assessment system* composed of a variety of assessment tools that include, but go beyond, tests.

At a minimum, a balanced English language proficiency assessment system should incorporate formative, interim, and summative assessments based on explicit linguistic expectations for each student. Balanced language assessment systems, as shown in Figure I.2, include:

- *Formative assessment*—an ongoing assessment process that occurs within instruction and provides students and teachers with feedback on students' progress toward specific targets in their language development. Language assessment for formative purposes can involve observation, student self-assessment, peer assessment and feedback, or teacher analysis of language samples. What is most important is that whatever is being analyzed, it is a naturally occurring part of the classroom learning activities and that the information is used to make helpful adjustments to instruction within the lesson.

- *Interim assessment*—a periodic assessment that provides students, parents, and educators with information on unit attainment or progress across units. Interim assessment can be seen as a short-cycled summative assessment.

- *Summative assessment*—an occasional (often annual) assessment that provides parents, educators, and policymakers with information on students' progress with regard to a course and/or standard. Examples of summative English language proficiency assessments are WIDA's ACCESS for ELLs, California's CELDT, and the TELPAS in Texas.

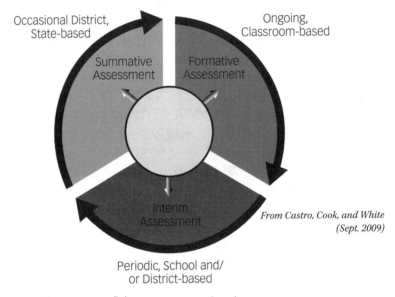

Figure I.2 A balanced language proficiency assessment system

What distinguishes these three types of assessments, then, are (a) the *grain size* of what is measured (specific targets, unit goals, or course goals and grade-level standards), and (b) the frequency of assessment, their varied degrees of proximity to instruction, and their impact on instruction. In formative assessment, students and teachers obtain and use information that changes instruction in the moment, rather than leading weeks or months later to changes in curricula or programs (Chappuis et al. 2011). Figure I.3 illustrates the relative frequency of assessment.

What unites a well-balanced language assessment system is continuity of purpose and coherence between learning targets and standards. At the heart of the balanced language assessment system are the same language standards that drive instruction. The assessment process is directly linked to an instructional target derived from these language standards in conjunction with content standards.

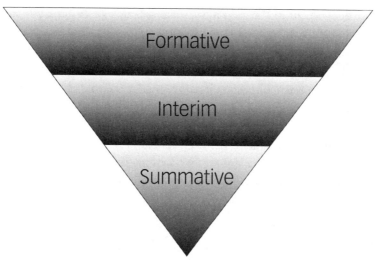

Figure I.3 The relative frequency of components of a balanced assessment system

A *balanced* language assessment system does not imply an equal number of tests of each kind, or that each assessment or test should carry the same weight within the broader system (Redfield, Roeber, & Stiggins 2008). What makes a language assessment system balanced is the correspondence of each component to the user's purposes. Mandated summative assessments are important and necessary for accountability purposes and for assessing the efficacy of programs or instructional models, but do not provide much actionable, evidence-based information about ELLs' actual language proficiency or content knowledge. In a balanced assessment system, summative tests are accompanied by periodic interim assessments and daily formative assessment activities to assure that ELLs' classroom instruction is tailored to their individual progress, giving students and teachers the opportunity to identify what students need to learn and to shape instruction to help them learn it.

The Process

In observing teachers as they engage in formative assessment practices, we have noticed the many creative ways they gather the information they need. We want to call attention to two kinds of variation. First, formative assessment varies in terms of the learning target. Some teachers may target content, language, or both at various points during instruction. A chemistry teacher can offer students feedback on their use of chemistry concepts in completing a laboratory exercise. Others may choose to combine the monitoring of chemistry concepts with a task that yields a language sample for analysis, so that the one activity serves as formative content assessment as well as an assessment of language for formative purposes.

Ideally, teachers plan and develop ways to assess language for formative purposes prior to a lesson and implement them at key points in the lesson. A journal entry assignment that invites students to self-assess their performance in mathematics is an example of formative assessment that may have been planned weeks before the semester started. Many other types of probes can be used at important junctures while students are working toward some end goal in a lesson or curriculum unit—some as simple as an exit card asking students to explain a concept or to draw the relationship between concepts. Many types of simple, brief activities can provide glimpses into students' current level of understanding in either content or language—planning a question-and-answer session during a lesson, observing students during an activity, or asking students to provide examples.

Formative assessment can also be spontaneous, immediate, and unplanned. While giving directions on how to perform a chemistry experiment, a teacher may recognize through her observation that some students do not understand that a reaction will occur when they mix the two chemicals and may decide to quickly review what a chemical reaction is. This would ensure that the students have the knowledge needed to comprehend what will occur and provide them with the language needed to express that knowledge—an example of spontaneous formative assessment and modification of instruction.

Regardless of whether it is planned or spontaneous, the goal of formative assessment is not to provide a grade. Rather, the goal is to provide teachers with the immediate feedback they need to adjust instruction and to provide students with the feedback they need to improve their learning. The goal of *language* assessment for formative purposes—our focus in this book—is to provide feedback to students and teachers so that students can take the next steps toward increasing their effectiveness in using English.

The Four Stages of Formative Assessment

The process we developed has four stages, as illustrated in Figure I.4. We explain these briefly here and in more detail in subsequent chapters.

- *Stage 1: Design and Teach.* The first stage involves designing and weaving a consistent focus on academic language into lessons, articulating clear language learning targets and objectives, and planning for the language assessment events. Chapter 1 will discuss this in more detail.

- *Stage 2: Sample Students' Language.* This stage involves building opportunities into lessons to gather samples of target language, a process we'll discuss in more detail in Chapter 1.

- *Stage 3: Analyze.* The third stage of the process involves analyzing students' language samples, using a set of lenses to help identify what is emerging in students' language, and considering how to adjust instruction, all of which will be discussed in Chapter 2.

• *Stage 4: Provide Formative Feedback.* The next stage, discussed in Chapter 3, is to give students clear, progress-oriented, and actionable information about their language use—both what they're doing well and what they can do to become more effective users of English—and to adjust instruction to meet students' needs, which brings us full circle to Stage 1. During formative feedback conversations, students and teachers plan together the next set of success criteria or targets and decide how to gather the next round of information. Chapter 4 provides examples of easily constructed tools that simplify data collection for formative assessment.

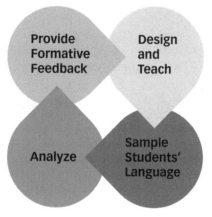

Figure I.4 The process for assessing language for formative purposes

Best Practices of the Assessment of Language for Formative Purposes: The IDEAL Model

Our observation of teachers in three school districts has helped us describe IDEAL language assessment for formative purposes. At its best, this type of language assessment has the five qualities (Castro, Cook, & White 2009) that are listed next.

It Is Integrated

Good language assessment for formative purposes is coherent with other language assessments in the school, district, and state. In other words, it shares the same language standards and language learning targets. The information gathered from all these sources can thus provide multiple lenses through which to view students' language development.

It Is Dynamic

Good language assessment for formative purposes is planned as part of the fluid instructional process, embedded in instruction, not distinct from it. This process results in language instruction that shifts and moves in response to information gathered through language assessment for formative purposes.

It Is Enlightening

The purpose of language assessment for formative purposes is to provide descriptive feedback to guide language instruction and development. Clear language learning targets make what students are aiming toward both explicit and specific. Students should have examples of what effective use of this new language should look or sound like, and both students and teachers need a shared understanding of the desired outcome.

It Is Attainable

Good language assessment for formative purposes fits well into the realities of classrooms and instruction, sampling and analyzing language during the regular flow of a lesson. If feedback is truly meant to shape instruction, the formative assessment process should not be something added after a lesson is planned, but should be planned as part of the natural flow of a lesson.

It Is Linked

Since students learn language best by putting it to important uses, good language assessment for formative purposes targets language that is integral to the content students are learning. Language learning targets should be shaped by students' emerging language abilities but, just as important, by the language demands of the content and the specific task as well. These links make the process relevant and authentic and ensure that the targets illuminate the path to academic success for ELLs.

The approach to integrated language assessment—the IDEAL model of language assessment for formative purposes used in this book—rests on two assumptions. First, ELLs are performing *double the work* of native English speakers in the country's middle and high schools (Short & Fitzsimmons 2007). To be successful in school—to graduate with a high school diploma, to enter an institution of higher education, or to find significant employment—ELLs must become proficient simultaneously in *both* the English language and the academic content of schooling. The challenges facing these students, their teachers, and their schools are substantial, especially for ELLs in the later grades who are working to assimilate abstract content and concepts with emergent English language skills, differing background knowledge, and, in some cases, with interrupted formal education. To meet these challenges, ELLs need immediate and systematic information about how the development of their language abilities is interacting with their academic performance.

Second, educators who serve ELLs in secondary schools need to continually build their knowledge and experience with second language acquisition, sheltered instruction, and differentiation, and to cultivate their ability to identify and teach the academic language and literacy of their content areas (Short & Fitzsimmons 2007). Teachers need practical strategies and knowledge to help learners develop the specific language abilities necessary to succeed in school (Bailey 2007; Bunch 2013).

Anyone who has observed a child knows that language, just like any other complex content, isn't learned all at once. Language learning is a process, and learners use tools like those we'll describe in this book to help them identify where they are in the process. These tools are a critical part of a tool kit for those who teach ELLs. Knowing where students are and where they need to end up helps teachers and students understand the direction and next steps to take. The resources in this book are designed to support that navigation along the path toward effectiveness with academic language.

How We Have Structured This Book

We have found that it is more effective to demonstrate good language assessment for formative purposes rather than to talk or write abstractly about it. To explain the cycle of formative assessment, we've chosen to show how it unfolds stage by stage in a school setting. In each of the following chapters, as we describe the steps in the cycle and introduce the tools teachers need, we will exemplify those steps by showing how a teacher might put the tools to work. To present the process in action, we provide a set of school, student, and teacher examples in subsequent chapters. Although the student language samples we provide are real, the setting and the characters themselves are fictitious, based on our collective experiences teaching ELLs in a variety of settings. Before we move on to explore the cycle in more detail, we'll introduce the schools, teachers, and students to help you visualize and apply the process.

The Schools

Just as ELLs are a very diverse group, so are the types of schools and instructional programs where they learn. In areas with high percentages of ELLs in each grade, school districts may have stand-alone programs that parallel the general education curriculum during the initial stages of ELLs' language development. Some districts have full bilingual education curricula. A very large percentage of ELLs in many states in the United States, however, are enrolled directly into mainstream classrooms and receive limited language support from specialist teachers who may either "push in" to the classroom, "pull out" students for separate language lessons, or co-teach with the content specialists. The variety of programs is a testimony to the creativity of teachers! We will situate the teachers and students in one of these latter, more typical and highly creative districts, where teachers use a variety of approaches to meet

ELLs' language learning needs in mainstream, English-only classrooms with limited support from English language specialists. The formative assessment cycle and the specific tools we'll share have been applied successfully across Grades 6–12, but to keep the "cast of characters" to a reasonable number, we'll situate all of the students in the same grade. We'll focus on three teachers and three seventh-grade students.

The Teachers

Jason Gardner is the English as a Second Language (ESL) teacher for the Metropolis School District, which has a small but growing number of ELLs. Jason's full-time position is shared among two elementary schools, one middle school, and one high school. Jason is a creative teacher who has developed several ways to meet the varied needs of his students. For students who are at the intermediate stage of English proficiency, he provides direct language instruction focused specifically on the academic language demands of various content areas. (Figure 2.2 in Chapter 2 shows a description of these English proficiency levels.)

For students whose English proficiency is at a lower level, Jason provides more frequent support, either through active collaboration with their classroom teachers (analyzing the language learning needs in the context of content lessons and developing strategies for integrated content-language instruction) or through co-planning and co-teaching occasional curriculum units with content specialists. This embedded and distributed professional development technique helps to increase the internal capacity of district faculty for integrated content-language instruction.

Kevin Davis is a seventh-grade history teacher. Kevin is new to the district, and this is the first year he has ELLs in his class. Three of the ELLs in his class are above intermediate level in proficiency, and one student, Kia, is new to the district. Kevin's work with Kia will be supported by Jason's frequent visits to the classroom, during which he will assist Kevin in delivering integrated content and language instruction. Twice a week during Kevin's planning time, he will meet with Jason to learn how to analyze the language central to his history lessons and develop strategies that integrate a focus on language development into his history lessons.

Elena Santos is a seventh-grade science and mathematics teacher. Because of her frequent collaboration with Jason during the past five years, she is accustomed to analyzing ELLs' language learning needs in science and mathematics and to building in instructional supports. She consults with Jason as needed, and she has offered to assist Kevin during his first year of differentiating instruction for ELLs.

The Students

Jorge was born near the border between Mexico and Texas in a community that spoke an indigenous language. He traveled with his parents as part of a migrant farm worker group, living and working in the Midwest from April through October, and returning to Texas for the rest of the year. His parents speak both Zapotec and Spanish and very little English. Like many ELLs, Jorge speaks several languages. He and his older brother can speak Zapotec, Spanish, and English. Last year, when Jorge entered the sixth grade, his parents found year-round jobs in the Metropolis School District and decided to settle there. Jorge was happy to stay in the same neighborhood and keep the friends he had recently made. Jorge is good-natured, well liked by teachers and classmates, and is a talented guitarist. Jorge's language proficiency level has not advanced from the intermediate level for the last three years. Although his language skills in listening and speaking are strong, his teachers have not had success in helping him use English more effectively in reading and writing, and, despite ESL support, he seems to be stuck.

Kia came to the United States four years ago at age nine when her family left Laos to join an aunt who had moved to the United States. Her family settled immediately in a neighboring town with an established Hmong community, where they continued speaking Hmong, with translation support provided by a few neighbors when needed. Kia entered school in third grade in a newcomers' English program that included intensive English language development, sheltered content classes, and acculturation of new students to the American school system. She spent less than a year in that program before her family moved to Metropolis, where ESL support is more limited. Kia's parents speak little English and have a limited understanding of the school system that serves Kia and her two older sisters and younger brother. Kia struggles in academic classes. Because she and her parents believe that education is critical for success, Kia has enrolled in an after-school program to improve her English. College students from the Hmong community staff the program, and Kia works primarily in English to learn how to use computers, playing games and managing a Facebook page.

Migdalia is a thirteen-year-old girl who was born in Caracas, Venezuela, who arrived in the United States one year ago. Her parents came to the United States as part of a church sponsorship program for immigrants. Back at home, her father was an engineer and her mother, who had completed a bachelor's degree, did not work outside of the home. In Venezuela, Migdalia attended private schools. She has strong literacy in Spanish and is a skilled writer, crafting short stories and poetry that she shares with her Spanish-speaking friends in Venezuela. Migdalia has many Spanish-speaking friends with whom she stays in touch via Facebook, but would like to have more friends who speak English. With much help from her father, who speaks both English and Spanish fluently, she is earning passing grades in core academic subjects. She tries hard to please her teachers, but school in the United States has been difficult for her in spite of her strong skills in English.

We'll follow these three students and teachers throughout the rest of this book, watching how the teachers embed formative assessment of language into their daily instruction and how students are engaged as partners in their learning.

1

Provide Formative Feedback

Design and Teach

Analyze

Sample Students' Language

Teaching and Sampling Academic Language: Weaving a Language Focus into Content Lessons

"Ongoing formative assessment by teachers can provide guidance to students which supports and extends their learning, encouraging deeper learning and development of transferable competencies."

—National Research Council (2012, p. 188)

Teachers and researchers alike have known for quite a while now that academic content and language are intertwined—after all, it would be difficult to teach a lesson without language! Language, either spoken or written, is the medium through which teachers and learners convey most ideas in classrooms. A picture may indeed be worth a thousand words, but even excellent diagrams, charts, pictures, videos, and other related means of conveying ideas can't stand alone. It's the discussion of these resources that gives meaning to them—and, indeed, without discussion about these resources, students may not understand them or use them effectively. Language matters, and ongoing efforts to help students learn the language they need, accompanied and supported by ongoing formative assessment of their progress, will help students succeed in the classroom and in situations beyond.

In this chapter, we'll discuss the importance of integrating a focus on academic language instruction and assessment into content lessons, and we'll give examples of how to do this in the lessons with the three students.

Academic Language

Many content teachers do not have the opportunity to study second language development and acquisition as a part of their teacher education or to receive specialized training to be effective teachers of the growing number of English Language Learners (ELLs) in their classrooms. Furthermore, those who have lived in English-speaking contexts all or most of their lives don't really notice language any more than we notice the sound of our hearts beating. Language is simply part of our world, and we don't usually have to pay much attention to it. We learned language so easily and so early that the experience of learning it is not part of our memory, although we may have some memory of struggling to learn some challenging new vocabulary in a physics course or calculus class. But for the most part, the rest of the language we learned—complex sentences and tightly packed clauses, chains of logical reasoning, how to pack a multitude of detail into concise phrases—was acquired without much attention to the elements or features of language. Similarly, we learned how to adjust language to fit particular contexts, including academic contexts; we wouldn't have been accepted into college or lasted through our first year there if we had not. We "cracked the code" of academic language easily because we had a solid foundation of years of exposure to and practice with English. But when we work with students who haven't yet cracked the code and who have not had the advantage of years of exposure to complex academic English, we need to bring language out of the background and pay attention to it.

So, where to start? Language, if you stop and think about it, is pretty complex and has many intertwined elements: vocabulary, phrases, sentences, different types of texts shaped by varied expectations and demands. Many people think that learning language is about learning vocabulary and grammar. But while these are important aspects of language, we're going to take a different approach, a *functional approach to language*, one that ties language learning to its purpose: creating meaning. We're going to show the systematic use of four lenses that focus attention on how language works to create meaning. We'll focus on what language does and on what students need to do with language in classrooms.

Weaving Academic Language Instruction into Lessons

Remember that we're focusing attention on the language students need to construct meaning—both internally, to themselves, and externally, with others—as they learn science or mathematics or English language arts or history. Because we view language instruction and formative language assessment as integral to content learning, not as add-ons, we want to demonstrate how teachers weave attention to language right into their other lessons. Let's take a moment to think about the strands that need to be woven into the lessons. We discuss these as five strands and approach them as guiding questions.

1. What are the particular language features we're going to focus on? What do those look like? What examples can I show my students?

2. Why is that feature important in this lesson? How does its use shape the meaning? Why did the writer do it that way? What are the pros and cons of that linguistic choice?

3. How can I capture this in achievable success criteria for my students?

4. What supports will students need to move toward this target?

5. What method or tool can I develop with my students to help us both monitor their practice with this new language and their growing content knowledge?

We'll take up these five questions in this and subsequent chapters, and we'll demonstrate through the examples what teachers do. But before we do this, we can't stress enough the importance of remembering that because students are the ones walking the path, they need to be involved every step of the way. It's not enough for teachers to know what students need to do; the expectations and the steps must be clear to students. We know what the end result needs to look and sound like, but students don't, so showing them what effective language looks like by clearly specifying success criteria helps them point themselves in the right direction and take the next steps toward increased effectiveness with language.

Where do we go to develop the success criteria to share with students? In a broad sense, success criteria come from learning progressions that articulate a thorough understanding of the content to be taught and of students' typical pathways through that content. They are based on an understanding of both the end goals of content instruction and of several typical stepping-stones along the way. Learning progressions have been developed for several disciplines, and that work is ongoing in the field of English language development. The English language development standards in use across the United States offer very broad, large-grained pictures of the English language development terrain. Although they vary across the United States, enough similarity exists across those standards to allow us to use, in this book, a set of Reference Performance Level Descriptors (RPLDs) that were developed to capture the major elements of all the English language development standards in use across the United States (Cook & MacDonald 2014). The RPLDs are shown and explained in more detail in Chapter 2. As the major reference point for stages of English development, they serve as the primary source of success criteria.

The RPLDs, and their more local equivalents from which they were derived, provide guidance about how language changes as students gain effectiveness with it. Some focus on the smaller bits of language, vocabulary and grammar. Others focus on larger chunks of language, clause and sentence changes and how those interact with both context and purpose. Regardless of which approach to language they follow, most performance-level descriptors are too large-grained to provide enough detail to guide instruction on a daily basis. For this reason, many teachers augment those with additional learning progressions and tools that offer a closer, more fine-grained look at some aspect of language. You will see examples of that in this book, as our exemplar teachers integrate success criteria derived from the RPLDs with other criteria related to the development of writing in specific genres. What's important about success criteria, whatever their source, is that they are used to guide a consistent movement toward a shared understanding of what effective language use looks and sounds like and to make that understanding clear to students.

It's important to talk with students about why we are focusing on the particular style of English that we call academic English. After all, students can express opinions, describe things, and explain how to do things quite well to their friends and families. Why should they learn to do it differently in school? This question, when taken seriously, opens up wonderful opportunities for teaching and learning. Talking about why chemists use a specific style of English and history writers use a slightly different style is an effective way to engage students in discussion about the deeply held values of certain academic disciplines. Write-ups of science procedures are organized in specific ways because scientists consider it important to relay a great deal of information logically and concisely, and they use the patterns common to our culture to do so. Scientific writing avoids personal pronouns, not to make the writing sound more formal but to make sure that the hard-won objectivity produced by careful adherence to the scientific process is reflected in the language used, and to maintain a consistent focus on the scientific phenomenon under study rather than on the people conducting the study. Successful students don't adopt the formal vocabulary and sentence patterns of an expert just to sound smart; rather, they take up this language to convey complex ideas more precisely and in ways that fit the expectations of their hoped-for professions. In other words, they learn to use the linguistic code of that profession. Engaging students in discussions about language choices gives teachers the opportunity to share with students the thinking patterns and values of academic disciplines, and it prepares students to take their place in the professional discourse communities they'll encounter in college and in the workplace.

In our experience, the assessment of language for formative purposes—even in the more spontaneous instances—doesn't happen by accident. When teachers build a language focus into lessons, it is also important to build in, right from the start, plans for ongoing language monitoring and feedback. As lessons progress, teachers have many natural opportunities to sample students' language, to assist students in self-assessment, to check students' progress, and to give them the feedback they need. But unless teachers plan for this in advance, these opportunities can go unnoticed, with an end result of cobbling together an add-on assignment or assessment after the fact.

As Heritage (2010b) has written, formative assessment is assessment *for* learning, not assessment *of* learning, and it needs to be part of the flow of instruction. Planning regular probes or checks into students' understanding and progress helps teachers adjust instruction to keep students moving forward. One way of strengthening the attention to ongoing assessment is to enlist students in this effort. Students who have helped to develop a tool to sample their progress toward language learning targets are likely to be both better motivated and better able to use that tool effectively. By enlisting students as collaborators in formative assessment, teachers help students develop important metacognitive skills and strategies and increase their buy-in into their own learning. We'll show how this works in more detail in Chapter 4, with the three sample teachers laying the groundwork in this chapter.

Putting the Tools to Work: Clarifying Genre Expectations

In this section, we'll show how teachers Elena Santos and Jason Gardner weave a focus on language instruction and formative assessment into Jorge, Kia, and Migdalia's lessons by focusing first on the genre in which the students will be working. The word *genre*, in the context of language learning and assessment, refers simply to patterns by which individuals organize and present information to others—not to the categories of literature in English Language Arts classes. Genres are very high-level organizing constructs of language, shaping both the specific sections of a message and the language structures and vocabulary used.

We focus on four broad genres, which capture most of what students write in classes, as well as their oral reports: Narrative/Recount, Report, Process/Procedure, and Argument. Each of these genres has specific components, and each component accomplishes a specific purpose: to introduce a topic, to summarize an argument, or to present an ordered list of events. These genres, and the components within them (shown in the second column of Figure 1.1), follow patterns that make it easy for a reader or listener to follow along. The way they unfold seems logical and natural to anyone who has grown up reading and hearing these patterned sequences, but there is nothing natural that shapes them other than many years of unspoken cultural agreements about how to present ideas to others. Different cultures, in which some ELLs have been raised, organize these four genres differently and may emphasize other genres in teaching and learning. Students not accustomed to the genre patterns common to American- or British-influenced cultures will need opportunities to engage meaningfully with commonly occurring genres in the United States to learn their patterns. These four main genres and their components are shown in Figure 1.1, informed by the work of Derewianka (1990).

Teaching students how to construct different genres occurs very naturally when teachers discuss writing reports in history or procedures in science. Teachers often show examples of well-written procedures, arguments, and reports and help students identify the distinct genre components such as introduction and sequence. When teachers go beyond simply showing students examples of good texts, however, and move into analyzing those texts with their students, students' understanding of language is deepened. Through analyzing what the example texts mean, whether or not they've been constructed effectively, and what makes them effective or not effective, students increase their awareness of the linguistic choices open to them.

Genres	Components Within Genres
Narrative/Recount to retell, or recall accounts or activities	**Personal/Imaginative Narrative** Setting Situation Complication or reorientation Resolution
	Factual Recount Orientation Account of events or actions May include explanation or justification Closing
Report to explain, give an account, or present details	Orientation/purpose Methods/activities Outcomes/results Discussion/conclusion
Process/Procedure to explain a natural or social process or procedure	Orientation/purpose Components/parts Instructions/sequences Outcomes
Argument to make a point, take a position, or present arguments	Statement of issue or position Reasons for issue/position Reasons against issue/position Summary of arguments Recommendation/restatement of position

Informed by Derewianka (1990)

Figure 1.1 Key academic genres and their components

Analyzing the language of discipline-specific texts provides an added benefit: When students analyze and talk about the language used to provide information about a content topic, they're also reviewing and discussing the content itself. Because language and content are inseparable, focusing on one sharpens students' focus on the other.

Let's look at how the three teacher examples build a focus on genre as an important organizing element of language into their lessons. When reading through these lessons, which are as complex as all lessons are, it is not necessary to remember all the elements. We'll include charts tracking each student's progress through the process, which we'll fill in as we go along, to demonstrate how the process unfolds.

Jorge in Elena Santos' Mathematics Class

Teacher Elena Santos is working with her students on solving two-step equations. As part of her ongoing attention to the clarity of students' thinking and to the Common Core State Standards (CCSS), she is planning to have the students explain to her, in writing, the procedure used to solve two-step equations.

> **CCSS.Math.Content.7EE.3.** Solve multi-step real-life and mathematical problems posed with positive and negative rational numbers in any form . . . convert between forms as appropriate; and assess the reasonableness of answers using mental computation and estimation strategies.

Starting with the content standard above, and adding in a focus on language, Elena identified this intended learning outcome.

> **Learning Objective:** Students will be able to solve two-step mathematical problems posed with positive and negative rational numbers. Students will write a clear procedure for this.

Overview of Lesson

Elena will have her students work in triads to solve the variable in an algebraic expression, providing them with manipulatives that include strings, plastic chips, and small trays to help them work through the problem. Since the start of the unit, the students have been adding the vocabulary items useful when solving equations (such as variable, coefficient, and equation) to a word wall.

1. After the group work, the class will come together as a group to discuss the different ways the triads solved the equations. The following day, students work again in groups, solving additional two-step equations using two different methods of their choice and then come together to present their chosen strategies to the whole group. As a class, the students discuss the pros and cons of each strategy, decide on the best procedure, and post it on the board.

2. After this activity, the teacher has the students work in pairs to read what their textbook says about solving similar equations. Students must compare the procedure they chose as a class to the procedure described in the book, decide which one they prefer, and then write in their mathematics journal a description of the best procedure for solving a two-step equation. As part of her formative assessment, Elena will circulate among her students, listening to their discussions and stepping in with suggestions or clarification as seems appropriate. Between this lesson and the next, she will analyze all of her students' written explanations of the procedure, checking both their mathematics knowledge and their writing progress in the Procedure genre and using relevant language effectively.

3. Following this, Elena will have her students work in their groups with additional equation types using activities similar to these, working out and expressing in writing procedures for each equation type.

Focus on Language

At the onset of this unit Elena posted a learning target that combined mathematics and language. Her content-based language target for all the students in the class is to write a clear and effective procedure explaining how to solve two-step equations. She plans to focus intensively on students' ability to explain in the Procedure genre. Students' ability to explain their actions and logic is important in all grades, but the expectations become more rigorous as students' progress through the grades, and Elena knows her students need to understand and practice writing procedures. She and her students have read several exemplars of well-written procedures on different topics in mathematics (converting fractions to decimals, dividing fractions), making note of how each genre component was developed and its purpose.

In the procedure that her students will write in their mathematics journals, Elena expects the following components: an orientation, sequence, and outcome. She knows that when students move from explaining a procedure orally, with easy reference to a visible model on the whiteboard or on their papers, to explaining a procedure with no visual reference at all, they tend to forget that the reader cannot see anything but their words. When the reader and writer do not have access to a shared drawing or object, *cohesion* (meaningfulness) requires that everything is presented and explained within the text, and that the connections within the text are clear to the reader. It's easy for the steps in a written sequence to get muddled quickly without a shared visual or physical referent, and Elena will listen and watch for this as she circulates among her students.

Because Elena knows that her students do better when they know what's expected of them, she has shown her students several examples of written procedures ranging from beginning level to excellent, and they have discussed these to identify what makes some procedures more effective than others. Together, Elena and her students developed the following *success criteria* related to writing an effective procedure:

- Provide enough detail so that each step is clear and easy for a reader to follow. Remember that your reader can't see anything but your words.

- Don't distract the reader with unnecessary information.

- Make the order of the steps clear.

- Make sure the reader can tell when you move from one step to another.

Because Elena has been working with Jason Gardner (the ESL teacher), her classroom is full of the meaning-making supports her students will need. She has learned to include strategies such as keeping a word wall of key vocabulary and doing more small-group and partner work to ensure her students have an opportunity to use academic language every day to build meaning together. Jason points out that since Jorge has excellent oral skills, he may work independently during Parts 1 and 2 of this lesson, but will need support for his writing in Part 3. Since both teachers (Elena and Jason) are present in the classroom during instruction, they decide to increase the instructional intensity and maximize writing support for students by setting up three stations. This allows them to organize students into three smaller groups, providing increased opportunities for interaction among the students and for more individualized teacher observation, feedback, and targeted support.

- *Station 1: Manipulatives.* One group will work with Elena, using manipulatives to explore several different ways to solve a two-step equation. She will support the group by scaffolding the conversation as needed, ensuring that they correctly use the new math vocabulary, and reminding them to take notes on the different solution strategies using a graphic organizer she has prepared.

- *Station 2: Reading and note-taking.* In this station, Jason will focus intensively on the genre expectations for procedure writing. He will observe and support students as they read the text and take notes, making the language of procedures explicit and co-creating with students the outlines they can use when they write their procedures. Jason and Elena work with the students to help them identify the genre components within the textbook procedure and to discuss these features before the students draft their outlines.

- *Station 3: Independent work.* A third station will be devoted to students working independently. Students at Station 3 will work on a computer program that allows them to interact with images on the screen to solve algebraic equations.

Following their completion of the three stations, the students will work independently to write the procedure for solving two-step equations in their mathematics journal, using their notes from the station activities and the word wall as guides to their writing.

Elena has two tutors who work with the students once a week on different days. Because these tutors also provide observation and targeted support, Elena involves them in the discussion of student work and subsequent modifications to instruction. She and the tutors will review students' mathematics journals and analyze the language samples provided by their first drafts of written procedures. They will use a tool created specifically for this purpose, which will be shown in Chapter 3, and will think about the formative feedback session they will have with each student.

Jorge's procedure, from his mathematics journal, is presented and discussed in Chapter 2. Figure 1.2 shows the first of the charts that track each student's progress. We'll keep filling these in as we go through the process with each child.

Lesson and Sampling	Grade 7 mathematics class, written procedure for solving two-step equations, sampled from math journal. Part of a longer unit in which students explore additional equation types, working out and writing procedures for each.
Genre	Procedure
Success Criteria	• Provide enough detail so that each step is clear and easy for a reader to follow. Remember that your reader can't see anything but your words. • Don't distract the reader with unnecessary information. • Make sure the reader can tell when you move from one step to another. • Make the order of the steps clear.
Language Sample	
Analysis	
Initial, Teacher-derived LLTs	
Formative Feedback Discussion	

(continues)

(continued)

Collaboratively Developed LLTs	
Tool to Collect Information	

Figure 1.2 Jorge's language assessment process

Kia in Kevin's Sheltered American History Class

Kevin teaches a *sheltered* social studies class for students who need language support. *Sheltered*, in this context, means that the class covers the same content as a non-sheltered class, but does it with reduced language demand and with a strong focus on embedded language instruction. Jason assists Kevin as he plans lessons, helping him build in language supports and making sure that the content he presents in this class is of the same cognitive rigor and meets the same content standards as his non-sheltered class.

In American History, Kevin's students are learning about the early stages of the formation of the United States. This week they have been reading and talking about the Constitutional Convention. One of the main goals of social studies instruction is to engage students in the examination of primary and secondary source materials to help them develop a critical understanding of historical events. For this unit, Kevin would like his students to examine the different positions of the delegates at the time of the Constitutional Convention. Kevin has chosen to address two standards through one learning objective in this unit, and he will focus ultimately on the Argument genre. During this early research phase of the unit, however, he will focus students' attention first on the Report genre.

Constitutional Convention: The Debate of the Century

CCSS.ELA-Literacy.RH.6-8.3. Identify key steps in a text's description of a process related to history/social studies (e.g., how a bill becomes law, how interest rates are raised or lowered).

CCSS.ELA-Literacy.W.7.2b. Develop the topic with relevant facts, definitions, concrete details, quotations, or other information and examples.

Learning Objective: Students will construct an argument for or against the signing of the constitution.

Overview of Lesson

Throughout the unit, students will be preparing for and engaging in a debate about the signing of the Constitution, representing different states and using primary and secondary sources as evidence. During the first part of the unit, students will conduct research and write a brief research report. Each student will be assigned a state, and will research that state's position during the Constitutional Convention, using some primary documents as well as written histories of their assigned states. The research will take place over several days, and both the reading and the writing will be challenging. To help his students clarify their thinking about events in history and develop their writing skills, Kevin provides regular opportunities for students to write, and to assess and reflect on their own writing. During this part of the unit, students will take notes and write brief research reports in their journals. Kevin will use these research reports as language samples, analyzing them for signs of student progress and development, and for guidance in planning the next steps in his instruction. Students will use these research reports when they enter the next stage of the lesson, preparing for the oral debates.

Focus on Language

For this unit, Kevin knows that reading primary and secondary source documents will be quite a stretch for students whose English language proficiency is below intermediate. So, for the research section he has worked with the librarian and media specialist at the school to find texts and online resources that are linguistically accessible to his students. He maximizes support by having students work in pairs in the library so that he can make use of the additional support of the library media specialist and her student assistant. To further support students' reading, he provides three-by-five inch cards with graphic organizers for students to enter their findings from various sources. Students will organize these cards by sorting or categorizing them by topic. Then, using the cards appropriate for their positions, students will draft written research reports. After receiving formative feedback on their reports, they will use them during the next stage of the lesson, preparing for the oral debates.

Kevin knows that many of the words Kia will encounter will be new to her. This occurs often when students read primary sources documents, and he suspects it will occur even more frequently for Kia. To help Kia continue to develop her vocabulary, Kevin has given her a list of a few words to pay particular attention to, and he has provided her with her own vocabulary journal where she writes down the meaning she derives from the context and other sources. She is learning to use reference materials and other sources to find the meaning of those words, and once a week she meets with Jason to review these. During that meeting they select three or four focus words that she tries to use during the following week. Both she and Kevin keep track of her use of these words and check in with each other at the end of the week.

Everyone in this sheltered history class has been learning and practicing the past tense of relevant verbs, because the past tense is pervasive in the sources they are researching. At the beginning of the week Kevin introduces a few verbs through shared reading, a strategy whereby the educator reads and students participate and discuss the ideas in the reading. In this case, students discuss the patterns in the verbs introduced and identify them in the reading. These are great opportunities to discuss language and compare English construction of the past tense to the students' home languages, thus helping students develop metalinguistic skills. The students are all working on developing longer and more varied sentences as well, and Kevin has provided some models of ways to combine ideas from two or three short sentences into one.

Throughout this unit Kevin will check frequent samples of his students' writing to see what progress they are making and to identify the next steps in their learning. The research summary he will check falls into the Report category on the genre chart (see Figure 1.1), and Kevin knows that reports in a subject like social studies typically include an orientation or purpose, a recounting of the events that occurred, and a statement about the outcome. Kevin has provided his students with sentence starters modeling each of these genre components.

Kevin and his students have discussed the following success criteria for their research reports:

• Summarize the important events and ideas.

• Do not re-tell everything you read.

A sample of Kia's first research report is provided in Chapter 2. Figure 1.3 shows Kia's process chart.

Lesson and Sampling	Grade 7 Sheltered Social Studies unit on the development of the U.S. Constitution, which will ultimately focus on the Argument genre. Early on, however, students are reading primary and secondary source documents about the Constitutional Convention and writing brief reports on their assigned readings. *Sample*: Report based on assigned reading.
Genre	Report
Success Criteria	Summarize the important events and ideas. Do not re-tell everything you read.
Language Sample	
Analysis	
Initial, Teacher-derived LLTs	

(continues)

(continued)

Formative Feedback Discussion	
Collaboratively Developed LLTs	
Tool to Collect Information	

Figure 1.3 Kia's language assessment process

Migdalia in Elena's Science Class

In science class, Elena's students have been discussing the scientific method as a tool for conducting research to answer important questions in science, applying the scientific method of inquiry in each unit. In this unit, students will focus on different energy sources, beginning with fossil fuels and moving into alternative sources of energy, as mentioned in the Next Generation Science Standard (NGSS) below.

> **MS-ESS3-4.** Construct an argument supported by evidence for how increases in human population and per-capita consumption of natural resources impact Earth's systems. [*Clarification Statement:* Examples of evidence include grade-appropriate databases on human populations and the rates of consumption of food and natural resources (such as fresh water, mineral, and energy). Examples of impacts can include changes to the appearance, composition, and structure of Earth's systems as well as the rates at which they change. The consequences of increases in human populations and consumption of natural resources are described by science, but science does not make the decisions for the actions society takes.]

> **Learning Objective:** Design and report on the use of the scientific method to test propulsion systems.

Overview of Lesson

Students will begin by reading and taking notes on a chapter about sources of energy. They will discuss the chapter in their small learning group, using the textbook and their notes to collectively answer these two questions: (1) What sources of energy were described? (2) What are the advantages and disadvantages of each type? Students will use the information that they read, but will also include their own experiences and opinions.

Elena will model the use of a software program (EngineSim) in which students can manipulate variables to design and test propulsion systems to determine which one is most efficient. Students will work in groups to run several simulations, conducting the experiment virtually, and will write a report explaining the application of the scientific method to their simulated experiment on propulsion systems. Elena will use the writing samples provided by these reports to assess students' progress in both conceptual understanding and in writing, and to guide her next steps in instruction. After students conduct and report on their virtual experiments, and receive formative feedback on their progress, they will design additional questions about different types of energy and propose ways to answer their questions using the scientific method.

Focus on Language

During their planning time, Jason and Elena discussed how to scaffold activities for students needing language support. Both agreed that Migdalia would be able to participate independently in all the activities, and that the unit provides an ideal opportunity to help Migdalia focus on writing for an academic audience. Migdalia loved writing in her classes in Venezuela. She is very creative and loves to write for dramatic effect; her poetry has been praised by several of her teachers. But she feels at a loss when it comes to writing the more formal papers she needs to write in her classes, papers that are supposed to show clearly and succinctly what she knows. Her grades are acceptable on those papers, but her teachers mention things like "the tone is a bit too personal" or "it needs to be tighter" or "it's not clear enough." Migdalia knows that the sentences she writes are correct most of the time, but does not know what sort of changes will improve her writing. In their initial conference about writing, Elena has told Migdalia that she can help her figure out what to work on. She knows that the writing style—the *voice*, or *register*—that is effective in writing about science is very different than that used in creative writing, and she will help Migdalia explore those differences. Together they will look at several writing samples and think about why the writer chose certain ways of expressing ideas over others.

Elena uses the physical environment to provide a rich language environment for her students, filling the walls with word lists, charts, graphs, and posters about language they can use during their writing. She also has binders with many examples of all common genres in science, ranging from poor to excellent, so that students can discuss and analyze the linguistic choices that make some reports more effective than others. Elena will focus on the exemplar reports with all students, and she will use two or three specific ones with Migdalia during their next conference.

The task of learning to write in a scientific style is a challenging one for many students, not only Migdalia, so Elena has designated every Friday as "Write Like a Scientist Day." Each Friday she spends fifteen minutes of the class talking explicitly about setting the tone in scientific writing. She provides models and brief interactive activities where students revise sentences from an informal tone to a more formal, objective one, and discuss where and when they might find that strategy helpful. For the rest of Friday's class, students are given time to work on their own writing assignments, provide peer assistance, and meet with the teacher. These "Write Like a Scientist" Fridays not only provide time for Elena to meet individually with Migdalia, but also provide the opportunity for Migdalia to meet with other students in a collaborative review session.

Migdalia is able to communicate detailed ideas through writing. She and Elena have discussed her next step in writing: working on writing more concisely and with a less personal, more objective voice. Elena meets with her to analyze the organization of what she has written, sometimes using highlighters of different colors to find the ideas or evidence supporting the main idea or argument. Often they draw a logic map onto the essay, using arrows to show the flow of ideas, and sometimes they actually cut up her writing and reorganize the pieces using a logic map or graphic organizer. For this particular essay, Elena provided Migdalia with a graphic organizer to organize and continue to develop the ideas for each step, while keeping the established sequence.

Elena knows that the components of this report should include a statement of the purpose, a description of the steps of the process, and a conclusion. Elena knows that Migdalia can convey this information effectively in a conversational tone, but now the task is to practice a different style of English that is more aligned with the expectations and values of science. Together, they write the following success criteria:

- Maintain an objective tone.

- Relay information efficiently and concisely. Try to combine related ideas into the same sentence to make it more efficient for your reader.

- Use connectors that make your logic clear to the reader.

Migdalia worked hard on her report, which is shared in Chapter 2. Figure 1.4 shows her process chart.

Lesson and Sampling	*Learning objective*: Design and report on the use of the scientific method to test propulsion systems. *Sample*: an early draft of a science report, written as part of a "Write Like a Scientist" day assignment.
Genre	Report
Success Criteria	Maintain an objective tone. Relay information efficiently and concisely. Try to combine related ideas into the same sentence to make it more efficient for your reader. Use connectors that make your logic clear to the reader.

(continues)

(continued)

Language Sample	
Analysis	
Initial, Teacher-derived LLTs	
Formative Feedback Discussion	
Collaboratively Developed LLTs	
Tool to Collect Information	

Figure 1.4 Migdalia's language assessment process

Final Thoughts: Gathering Samples of Students' Language

As these examples demonstrate, language and content are so closely related that weaving a focus on language into mathematics, history, and science need not add extra steps. Keeping track of students' developing language can occur simultaneously with tracking their developing content knowledge. There's no need to create new assignments to obtain samples of student language; language samples can be gathered during lessons.

Formative assessment is not about working harder; it's about working strategically to attend to the language learning opportunities that are part of every lesson. Teachers, we realized during our work in several school districts, can easily find language samples in student journals, exit card activities, two-minute essays, or homework assignments. Using everyday examples of students' language, rather than planning extra assessments, makes it easy to embed into daily instruction the frequent monitoring and guidance that is the heart of the formative assessment process.

Our description of this process is not intended to be prescriptive; the formative assessment process is fluid and adaptable. Once familiar with the process and the resources, teachers use the resources when needed and often have all the stages in mind throughout a lesson. This enables teachers to notice and take advantage of the opportunities that present themselves as they work with students.

2

Provide Formative Feedback

Design and Teach

Analyze

Sample Students' Language

Where Are We and Where Are We Going? Analyzing the Data and Identifying Language Learning Targets

"Instruction must be aimed not so much at the ripe as at the ripening functions …"
—Lev Vygotsky
(1986, p. 188)

Gathering evidence of students' language performance, as discussed in the previous chapter, is an important step. But unless we know how to make sense of the data and relate it to a model of language development, all we're left with is a more sophisticated list of what a student is, and is not yet, doing proficiently. Formative assessment involves analyzing language samples against a set of guidelines, identifying the next likely steps in language growth, sharing that information with students in ways that support their growth, and then planning the next steps to keep students moving forward.

In this chapter we will take up the important topics of analyzing student language samples and re-setting *language learning targets* to guide instruction. We will present three more lenses (text structure/organization, grammatical forms, and vocabulary) through which to examine language, adding these to the lens of genre focus (discussed in Chapter 1). We'll also introduce the *Performance Level Descriptors* (PLDs) that summarize the characteristics of students' language at each of three levels, which will serve as a model for analyzing language development. The levels described by the PLDs are very broad and not as fine-grained as we wish for this purpose. The FLARE project, on which this book is based, used a model of language development based on the linguistic complexity of certain language functions common in secondary education. An additional model of language development for the elementary grades, the Dynamic Language Learning Progression (www.dllp.org/), is being developed. Currently, what most teachers have available are PLDs, so we will use those as a model to guide the analysis of students' language.

We'll discuss the three lenses, and in the final section of the chapter we'll model their use in the classrooms of teachers Jason, Kevin, and Elena.

Four Lenses for Language Analysis

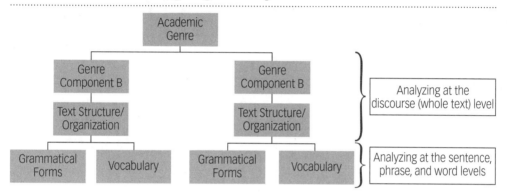

Figure 2.1 Four lenses for language analysis: academic genre, text structure/organization, grammatical forms, and vocabulary

Figure 2.1 shows the relationship of our four lenses to one another in our analysis of students' language samples. At the broadest level of analysis, we consider the effectiveness of the entire text—the genre and its components. Next, we consider how well the text is organized or structured in relation to the expectations for that academic genre. Finally, we move to smaller grain size if we need to, analyzing particular features of students' use of grammatical structures and vocabulary or word choices.

Performance Definitions

As we mentioned above, the analysis of student language involves comparing it to an accepted model of academic English development. We will use PLDs, since those are available to most teachers. Every state has a document that articulates standards for English language proficiency development and shows how language changes as students progress from one level to another. All PLDs are based on some model of English language development, and across the United States they vary primarily in degree of specificity and number of levels. For our purposes here, we will use the Reference Performance Level Descriptors (Cook & MacDonald 2014) derived from an analysis of PLDs across several states and language assessment consortia. Figure 2.2 shows the RPLDs.

RANGE OF PERFORMANCE IN ENGLISH: Descriptors reflect performance at exit stage of each level

	PRODUCTIVE			RECEPTIVE		
	Low	Moderate	High	Low	Moderate	High
ORAL	Engages in basic oral interactions in direct informational exchanges on familiar and routine subjects; Uses repetitive phrasal and sentence patterns with formulaic structures common across discipline areas; Uses frequently occurring, commonly used words and phrases	Engages comfortably in most academic discussions on familiar topics; expresses feelings, needs, and opinions using extended discourse; Uses a variety of sentence structures with varying complexity; Uses specific and some technical content-area vocabulary and expressive words or phrases	Produces, initiates, and sustains extended interactions tailored to specific purposes and audiences on a variety of social and academic topics; Uses a variety of sentence structures and varied levels of complexity tailored to the communicative task; Uses a range of abstract, specific, and technical content-related vocabulary; uses a range of idiomatic expressions and words or phrases with multiple meanings	Understands simple or routine directions and short, simple conversations and discussions on familiar topics; Demonstrates an understanding of repetitive phrases and simply-constructed sentences across subject areas; Demonstrates an understanding of words and phrases from previously learned content material	Comprehends most academic discussions on familiar topics and follows discussions related to feelings, needs, and opinions in extended discourse; Comprehends a variety of grammatical constructions and sentence patterns common in spoken language in academic and social contexts; Understands specific and some technical content-related vocabulary, some idiomatic expressions, and words or phrases with multiple meanings	Comprehends longer, elaborated directions, and extended conversations and discussions on familiar and unfamiliar topics in academic and social contexts; Comprehends a wide variety of complex and sophisticated sentence structures in varied academic and social interactions; Understands a wide range of specific, technical, and idiomatic words and phrases; comprehends words and phrases with multiple meanings

TEXT-BASED	Produces basic written statements (text) in directed tasks or activities on familiar and routine topics Produces simple and expanded sentences Uses high-frequency and common learned vocabulary and phrases drawn from academic content areas	Produces text that expresses ideas to meet most social and academic needs Produces text that reflects a grasp of basic grammar features and sentence patterns with evidence of emerging use of more complex patterns Uses specific and some technical content-related vocabulary, some idiomatic expressions, and words or phrases with multiple meanings	Expresses ideas to meet a variety of social needs and academic demands for specific purposes and audiences Produces text using a variety of grammatical structures and a broad range of sentence patterns matched to purpose Uses a range of abstract, specific, and technical content-related vocabulary; uses a range of idiomatic expressions and words or phrases with multiple meanings	Demonstrates an understanding of simple sentences in short, connected texts with visual cues, topic familiarity, and prior knowledge Exhibits a growing understanding of basic, routinely used English language structures in content-area texts Understands frequently occurring content words and phrases in content-area texts	Demonstrates comprehension of increasingly complex texts; identifies detailed information with fewer contextual clues on unfamiliar topics Demonstrates comprehension of a variety of complex grammatical constructions and sentence patterns in content-area texts Understands specific and some technical content-related vocabulary, some idiomatic expressions, and words or phrases with multiple meanings	Comprehends a variety of complex texts and identifies general and detailed information in familiar and unfamiliar texts and topics Comprehends a wide variety of complex and sophisticated sentence structures from varied academic and social sources and contexts Understands a wide range of specific, technical, and idiomatic words and phrases; comprehends words and phrases with multiple meanings

Figure 2.2 Performance-Level Descriptors

These RPLDs show three broad levels of language proficiency, and within each level they show the characteristics of students' language in relation to three bulleted items:

- *Text structure or organization*—the amount of language that students can process or produce, as well as their ability to use language to link ideas coherently and cohesively

- *Grammatical forms*—students' ability to use grammatical moves to combine sentences, to structure dependent or hierarchical relationships to create precise relationships between ideas, to embed phrases or clauses within other sentences or clauses to express ideas concisely

- *Vocabulary usage*—the sophistication of students' word choices, ranging from general everyday words to more specific words related to academic content, to very technical and unusual words, and the ability to create precise and finely nuanced meanings through word choices.

Studying students' writing or transcripts of their speech with these variables in mind can help us roughly gauge a student's English language proficiency to help us understand, in a broad sense, where students are in their language development. Of course, there are formal, standardized summative assessments that provide this kind of information, but for instructional purposes we need current information. Using the performance definitions as a broad indicator of language proficiency, we are able to get a rough estimate of where a student's current growth point is in relation to the overall language learning trajectory.

The performance definitions are organized into four quadrants:

1. Productive-Oral, or speaking

2. Productive-Text, or writing

3. Receptive-Oral, or listening

4. Receptive-Text, or reading

We often find that a student is not at the same proficiency level in all areas. We will need to remember this and focus our attention on the relevant section as we analyze students' oral or written language samples.

Analyzing Language

As we demonstrated in the previous chapter, we can obtain examples of student language as part of regular lessons. But once we have them, where do we start to analyze something as complicated as language? Any language, spoken or written, is like a complex machine, with many parts interacting. If any one part is out of sync with the others, the message may become lost, so the reader or listener may have to work hard to decipher it. If that happens, where do we start? Do we focus on the small bits—the words? Or do we focus on syntax and try to find and fix any errors there? Or do we analyze the discourse level—the whole message at once?

Aided by our interaction with many teachers, we've fine-tuned a procedure and method of analysis that offers answers to these questions. Figure 2.3 shows the procedure that we'll describe. We will apply this procedure to three samples of student writing later in this chapter.

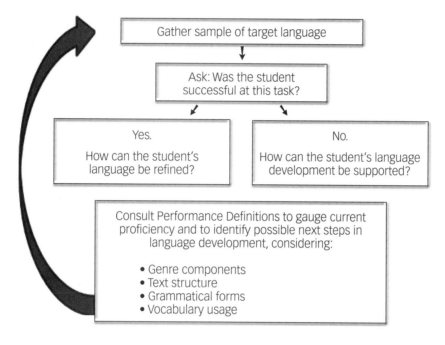

Figure 2.3 Systematic language analysis

The first question we ask in analyzing the language samples we've gathered is whether or not the student was successful at the task assigned. This focuses attention on the student's use of language to achieve a purpose and calls us to attend to effectiveness before considering correctness. Remember that we're most concerned with student content learning, as supported by their language. ELLs, by definition, have not yet developed full proficiency in academic English, so focusing on correctness—on those things they cannot yet do perfectly—provides little useful information. ELLs can and do express important and complex ideas correctly and effectively long before they become proficient in their use of English, so focusing on their overall effectiveness first, and on linguistic correctness later and as it relates to their meaning-making, is a more positive and productive approach.

If the student's communication was effective, we consider ways to introduce a new element of language for students to practice. If the student's communication was not very effective, we consider which language features to focus on to help the student clarify the communication of his or her idea. In either case, our interest is in helping students communicate their ideas more effectively.

Effectiveness depends in part on how well a message is tailored to its purpose and context. This interaction of linguistic choice and context is captured in the following questions that we use to guide our analysis:

1. Genre components: Did the student include and effectively organize the necessary components? Was any part missing? Was the specific purpose of each component (for example, to tell the sequence of events or to identify what caused what in an experiment) achieved effectively? Did the explanation contain any extraneous information that would have been better left out? Was the organization appropriate to the context, in terms of formality, brevity, and objectivity? Does the degree of formality or informality match the context?

2. Text structure and organization: Are there relationships among ideas that the student seems to be trying to express? Was the student successful at linking ideas to convey the underlying logic of his or her explanation? Was the student able to express ideas concisely and compactly, or are the ideas relayed in a conversational pattern of many short, linked sentences? Does the language chosen match the context? Is it too dense and compact for listeners to follow easily, or is it so informal and lengthy that it is inefficient for readers to follow?

3. Grammatical forms: Does the student correctly form the phrases, clauses, and sentences he or she uses? Are there signs that the student is attempting new language structures?

4. Vocabulary usage: Has the student used the type of vocabulary expected for this assignment? Is the student using words that create precise meanings, or is precision dependent on lengthy descriptions in lieu of precise vocabulary? Are there signs that the student is trying to use knowledge of English word formation strategies to expand his or her vocabulary? Would learning synonyms or hyponyms be helpful here?

Although each of these four lenses may highlight information our students could act on, we often find that one particular lens brings the greatest clarity to our analysis, identifying either the strengths of a student's language, the features that seem to be changing, or the aspects with which a student needs additional support. Determining a student's strengths in all features of language helps teachers identify constructive next steps.

Setting Language Learning Targets That Relate to Success Criteria

Given how important it is that students know where they're headed, let's spend a moment reviewing the points made earlier about success criteria. Depending on the level of detail provided by the learning progression or progressions we work with, our initial success criteria may be very broadly defined, as was the case with our three exemplar students. We want to guide our students toward a desirable end goal, but until we have had a chance to look closely at the language they use, we may not be able to be more specific about their next steps. Once we have had a chance to analyze their language use more closely, however, we can develop more focused objectives. In our process, we call these *language learning targets* (LLTs), which are analogous to what some might call learning objectives. Good LLTs share characteristics with good formative feedback, which you'll read more about in Chapter 3. LLTs state clearly, simply, and specifically what students should be working toward in their language development—for example, "Put the details of time and place in your history report into prepositional phrases" or "Revise these sentences to keep the scientific construct in sentence-first position." LLTs are not vague statements encouraging students to "make this clearer"; whenever possible, LLTs are specific about the actual language that students need to practice.

As we consider the important questions related to the four lenses, we also need to be ready to share this information with students. Formative assessment is not about what we teachers know. It's about putting that knowledge into our students' hands and making sure it leads to action. The most effective LLTs are those developed collaboratively by teachers and students. The process of setting language learning targets is not complete until the student has been brought into the conversation (the focus of the next chapter). Before we take up that topic, however, we want to address some interesting questions that arise when teachers think about sharing information and developing LLTs with students. Analyzing students' language use and progress consistently leads back to questions about how to teach.

- *How much information should I show my students?* Target setting is not complete until the student is brought into the loop. We know that students do best when they know where they are headed and why they're doing what they're doing. The next chapter provides some examples of the types of discussions teachers can have with students. How much information from the analysis to give students is a decision best made on an individual basis. Some students will benefit from reviewing the whole process. Others, perhaps less confident, may find too much information daunting and might be better motivated by being shown only the most relevant sections. What is essential is that we give students timely, clear, specific, actionable information that will help them change their performance.

- *Will I have different LLTs for every student?* In a large class there will likely be groups of students with similar targets, enabling teachers to address their learning needs in small group settings. Sometimes sorting those learning needs by language feature can help organize the group work. Five students may be working on tightening up their writing and making it more concise (text structure), while others are working on specific types of sentence-level features (grammatical forms) such as prepositional phrases or correct verb tenses, while a small group is working to master content vocabulary (vocabulary usage).

- *How do I fit LLTs into my lesson planning?* Once targets are developed in collaboration with students, teachers further engage students in deciding how to assess movement toward those targets. Together, teachers and students think about what tool or method will help to quickly and easily capture the information needed. As demonstrated in Chapter 1, language instruction and assessment can be integrated into a content lesson, rather than being "add-ons." When teachers remember that students are unable to access content without understanding its language, the interweaving of content and language instruction and assessment makes good sense—and good teaching.

Writing Samples, Analyses, and Identification of LLTs

So what does the process of setting LLTs look like? Let's consider the language that emerged in the lessons described at the end of Chapter 1. As we revisit each of the classroom scenarios, we model the process of learning from students' language use using the system we shared earlier (see Figure 2.3). In this way we can analyze their language samples, thereby identifying their language strengths and needs and possible next steps in their language learning.

Analyzing Jorge's Language Sample

Jorge had to explain how to solve a two-step equation in writing in his mathematics journal, an example of a procedure. Elena had her students develop a procedure to solve two-step equations, and then work in pairs to read what their textbook had to say about solving these equations. After comparing the procedure they had devised to the procedure described in the book, they were to choose their preferred method and clearly describe that procedure in their math journals. As part of her formative assessment (content and language), Elena planned to analyze all of her students' written procedures to check both their math knowledge and their effective use of language.

Here is what Jorge wrote:

Two. Step. Equation. Essay.

In solving a two step equation problems the first step would be Isolating your variable. and some evidence would be having a variable next to the number. then you inverse the operation. and what happens to one side you do to the other side. and you get rid of the coeifficient the number with the variable. and when your done solving the problem you check your answer. and an example we did as a group was 3n–6=15 and the steps for solving this problem is you Box the number with the variable, then you Inverse of operation and the last step you do is divide. alsotheise problems are very easy to solve an sometimes hard to solve. and another example we did as a group was 5–x=17 and that problem was kind of hard to solve but the tutors showed us how to solve it step by step

Learning from Jorge's Writing

Using the procedure illustrated in Figure 2.3, Elena asks herself whether Jorge was successful at the assigned task. Since Elena was using this task to assess Jorge's knowledge of the mathematical procedure, we need to consider whether Jorge's writing is effective at conveying his understanding of the procedure, or whether it leaves Elena wondering. In this case, Elena is left wondering. It's clear that Jorge has learned some of the operations in the procedure (isolating a variable, using an inverse operation), and his use of transition words shows a logical sequence of mathematical operations. But Jorge's writing is not clear enough for her to know exactly what he's referring to in some of some steps.

To decide how to help Jorge explain this procedure more effectively, Elena needs to apply the four lenses described earlier. Although she's tempted to jump ahead to what she thinks could be the most relevant language feature for Jorge, she has learned that going through the analysis in order helps her notice things she might otherwise have missed. She focuses her attention first of all on the *genre components* needed in an effective procedure. Has Jorge included an orientation or statement of purpose, the necessary steps, and a closure? Elena decides that yes, the first half of Jorge's first sentence does orient the reader to the purpose, and the use of "the first step" and "then" early on leads the reader through the first few steps, but the steps are less clearly demarcated after that and there is no clear closure to the explanation. Elena also notes that Jorge has included his personal reaction in this written explanation, something that is always interesting to a teacher, but which has no part in a write-up of a mathematical procedure. In Jorge's case, she is more interested in the way he describes the mathematical constructs and entities in his writing. His use of terms such as "the number" and "the operation" and "some evidence" leave the reader wondering, "What number? What operation? Some evidence of what?" This is a common problem for students learning to use writing to express ideas about abstract entities without visible referents. Elena concludes that Jorge has included the necessary genre components but has not accomplished their purposes effectively.

What about *text structure*? Is Jorge's writing well organized and coherent? Elena notes Jorge's use of "and" to demarcate and sequence steps in the procedure—a strategy for connecting ideas common in conversation but that is not very effective in demarcating the separation between steps. Are the logical connections between the ideas made clear? Jorge does give a hint of his reasoning when he says, "what happens to one side you do to the other side," but the referents of "one side" and "the other side" are unclear, and the logic becomes muddled. This, combined with the lack of clear demarcation and sequencing of the steps of the procedure, leaves Elena uncertain of Jorge's knowledge of the procedure.

What about *grammatical forms*? It's possible that Jorge is trying to use a variety of syntactic structures in his writing, including what could be compound and complex sentences, but the punctuation he's used makes this difficult to know. It's clear to Elena that Jorge needs to work on sentence formation, capitalization, and punctuation in order to make his ideas clear.

What about *vocabulary usage*? Elena thinks that Jorge has done well in this area. Jorge has used the specific vocabulary terms *isolate*, *variable*, *coefficient* correctly, but misuses *inverse* as a verb ("You inverse the operation.").

Elena estimates that Jorge is currently writing at a low proficiency level, based on his emerging use of varied sentence forms. She does not yet see the emergence of any intermediate level features. Elena feels comfortable with her decision to focus instruction at sentence-level features in the LLTs she will develop.

Setting Jorge's Preliminary LLT

Where should Elena focus her instruction to help Jorge express his ideas more clearly? What are some possible LLTs for Jorge? Having looked at Jorge's writing through these four lenses, Elena has noticed that each lens has brought into focus ways in which Jorge could increase his effectiveness with language. All areas will ultimately need attention, but which focus will be most effective now?

Elena decides to focus attention at the discourse level, rather than on the smaller bits of language. As much as errors in capitalization and punctuation jump out at a reader and distract from the message, Elena knows that even if those were corrected, Jorge's meaning would still not be clear, and it is Jorge's need to convey his meaning more effectively that drives her decision. She will focus first on helping Jorge master the expectations of the Procedure genre (specifically, the inclusion of all and only relevant sections) and on helping him increase his clarity in describing abstract constructs not visible to his reader. In working on these, she and Jorge will, of course, touch on writing conventions such as punctuation and capitalization to make intended meanings clear to readers. Because Elena's experience has shown her that students find a focus on clarifying their meaning much more energizing than focusing solely on smaller details, she will embed the discussion of those details within the larger purpose. She wants Jorge to be an active partner in this work and for him to experience being a capable learner. Figure 2.4 shows Jorge's language assessment process.

Elena's preliminary LLTs for Jorge include the following:

1. Make your descriptions clear to readers who can't see your computations. Think carefully every time you use a pronoun (it, that one, the other one) and ask yourself whether the reader will know what you're referring to.

2. Remove any details that aren't part of the genre components for a procedure.

Lesson and Sampling	Grade 7 mathematics class, written procedure for solving two-step equations, sampled from math journal. Part of a longer unit in which students explore additional equation types, working out and writing procedures for each.
Genre	Procedure
Success Criteria	Provide enough detail so that each step is clear and easy for a reader to follow. Remember that your reader can't see anything except your words. Don't distract the reader with unnecessary information. Make sure the reader can tell when you move from one step to another. Make the order of the steps clear.
Language Sample	**Two. Step. Equation. Essay.** In solving a two step equation problems the first step would be Isolating your variable. and some evidence would be having a variable next to the number. then you inverse the operation. and what happens to one side you do to the other side. and you get rid of the coeifficient the number with the variable. and when your done solving the problem you check your answer. and an example we did as a group was 3n–6=15

(*continues*)

(continued)

Language Sample *(con't)*	and the steps for solving this problem is you Box the number with the variable, then you Inverse of operation and the last step you do is divide. alsotheise problems are very easy to solve an sometimes hard to solve. and another example we did as a group was 5–x=17 and that problem was kind of hard to solve but the tutors showed us how to solve it step by step
Analysis	*Strengths*: It's clear that Jorge has learned some of the operations in the procedure (isolating a variable, using an inverse operation) and has used some transition words to show the sequence of mathematical operations. *Genre components*: Jorge has used a brief orientation statement. There is evidence of an attempt to sequence steps. There is no clear closure. An unnecessary component has been included: a personal opinion, with a related example. *Text structure or organization*: The text is not structured to suit its purpose of providing information in the absence of visual referents. The demarcation between steps is unclear after the initial steps. *Grammatical forms*: Jorge may be attempting to use more varied language structures, but errors in punctuation and capitalization make this difficult to discern. *Vocabulary*: Jorge has used several content-specific terms (*isolate*, *variable*, *coefficient*) accurately and has used one term (*inverse*) incorrectly as a verb.
Initial, Teacher-derived LLTs	Make your descriptions clear to readers who can't see your computations. Think carefully every time you use a pronoun (*it*, *that one*, *the other one*) and ask yourself whether the reader will know what you're referring to. Remove any details that aren't part of the genre components for a procedure.

(continues)

(continued)

Formative Feedback Discussion	
Collaboratively Developed LLTs	
Tool to Collect Information	

Figure 2.4 Jorge's language assessment process

Analyzing Kia's Language Sample

Kia's language sample comes from the brief research report she wrote after reading about her assigned state's position regarding the Constitutional Convention. Kia had to read both primary and secondary source documents and write a report that met the following success criteria.

- Start your report with an orientation, tell the important activities that occurred, and end by telling the outcome.
- Include all the important ideas.
- Use the sentence frames as models for two new sentences.

Here is Kia's research report:

> Piledafea, shermon become with the plan of the consititution.
>
> All of the people in the united states had to vote for a new consititution so that people and their slaves would have their natural rights.
>
> The meeting at phildaphe, the 9 states had to vote for a new consititoion. Then the farmers come destoryed about everyting of the government

Learning from Kia's Writing

The first question Jason asks himself when looking at Kia's writing is, "What did Kia do well?" There is almost always something in any student's writing that can be refined, but Jason knows he gets further working from students' strengths than from their deficits. In this sample of Kia's writing, Jason sees that Kia has captured some essential concepts from her research: the name of one of the delegates from Connecticut (Sherman), the fact that there were nine slave states, that the meeting occurred in Philadelphia, and that people had to vote on the constitution. In addition, she has used all three of the vocabulary words they had focused on (*constitution, vote,* and *government*) in ways that suggest she has grasped their meaning in this context, and she has attempted to model new sentences after the sentence starters Jason had provided. While noting these positive signs, Jason also notes that Kia's ideas were not clear to him.

Finding Kia's Starting Point

Jason usually starts by considering a student's understanding of the genre and *genre components*. Although Jason does not have a clear understanding of the ideas Kia was attempting to present, he is pretty clear that the essential *genre components* of orientation, sequence of events, and conclusion are not present. Kia has described some purposes or events, but Jason doesn't have enough understanding of Kia's ideas to evaluate whether she has sequenced these correctly, so will meet with her to assist her in explaining her thinking further. Considering Kia's writing in terms of *text organization, grammatical forms*, and *vocabulary usage*, Jason decides that Kia is currently writing at a low proficiency level. (See Figure 2.2 for a description of English proficiency levels.) This supports his thinking that the language needed to write a clear summary is beyond Kia's independent reach right now, and that his idea to provide sentence starters was a good one. After he has a clearer idea of what Kia is attempting to say, he will think about what additional or alternative supports might help her express her ideas more effectively. Jason will continue to provide Kia with information about and examples of short but effective reports to help her learn the genre patterns she will encounter and eventually use. But for now he and Kia will focus their attention primarily at the word- and sentence-level features of language to help Kia practice those essential "building blocks."

Setting Kia's Preliminary LLT

Given Kia's emerging ability with grammatical forms, Jason is impressed that, in addition to using the sentence frame provided (sentence 2), Kia has attempted three additional sentences without frames. It is unusual for Kia to take risks with language, and Jason sees her willingness to experiment as a very positive sign. Similarly, he notes her movement beyond simple sentences, specifically her use of prepositional phrases to incorporate detail into sentences. It seems that she may also have attempted to use one at the onset of sentence 3, but perhaps is not sure she can begin a sentence with a prepositional phrase. Jason wants to support this emerging feature in Kia's language, and he tentatively plans a focus on prepositional phrases as Kia's next LLT since they are often used to add important details of time and place when writing about history. Additionally, he recognizes that he will need to provide direct instruction, graphic organizers, exemplars, and more modeling to help Kia learn to summarize.

Jason's Preliminary LLTs for Kia

Although Jason knows he'd like to work on prepositional phrases with Kia next, he decides that he has to wait to draft LLTs until he has spoken with Kia. He needs to know more about what she was trying to accomplish in the sentences she wrote and what ideas she was trying to express. He is not certain that she understood the reading she was assigned, and he may need to add in some LLTs related to reading comprehension. In the next chapter, we'll relate his conversation with Kia and the LLTs they crafted collaboratively.

Kia's language assessment process is shown in Figure 2.5.

Lesson and Sampling	Grade 7 Sheltered Social Studies unit on the development of the U.S. Constitution, which will ultimately focus on the Argument genre. Early on, however, students are reading primary and secondary source documents about the Constitutional Convention and writing brief reports on their assigned readings. *Sample*: Report based on assigned reading.
Genre	Report
Success Criteria	Summarize the important events and ideas. Do not re-tell everything you read.
Language Sample	Piledafea, shermon become with the plan of the consititution. All of the people in the united states had to vote for a new consititution so that people and their slaves would have their natural rights. The meeting at phildaphe, the 9 states had to vote for a new consititoion. Then the farmers come destoryed about everyting of the government
Analysis	*Strengths*: Kia has captured some ideas from the reading, has used three new vocabulary words, and has attempted new sentence structures. *Genre and genre components*: Not present *Text structure or organization*: She has used sentence frames, linking ideas with "so that" to express purpose. *Grammatical forms*: She has used sentence frames for sentence 2 to link clauses, and she may have attempted prepositional phrases in sentences 1 and 3. *Vocabulary*: Several word choices are confusing.
Initial, Teacher-derived LLTs	Teacher decides to wait until she meets with Kia to formulate these.

(continues)

(*continued*)

Formative Feedback Discussion	
Collaboratively Developed LLTs	
Tool to Collect Information	

Figure 2.5 Kia's language assessment process

Analyzing Migdalia's Language Sample

Migdalia's language sample is the draft of her research report that she wrote in Elena's science class. Using software that allowed them to simulate propulsion experiments, groups of students ran several simulations to conduct the experiment virtually, and they were tasked with writing reports explaining the application of the scientific method to their simulated experiment on propulsion systems. Here is what Migdalia wrote:

Steps to the Scientific Method

There are six steps of the Scientific Method that scientists use to help them make investigations. First, they ask a scientific question that is not based on opinion, but can be tested. The next step is to form a hypothesis that is a possible explanation to a scientific question that could be based on their observations. The third step is to design an experiment by testing the factor in the scientific question. In this case, the variables being tested are the type of propulsion system and how it's affecting fuel efficiency. Scientists also have to keep the factors the same between the two things that they're testing. Later, scientists collect data include the observations, data tables and graphs. Fifth, they analyze the results by comparing the data. Finally, the last step is to draw a conclusion to see whether or not the hypothesis was supported In summation, the scientific method is a helpful tool for scientists to use in their experiments.

Finding Migdalia's Starting Point: Using the Performance Definitions

Learning from Migdalia's Writing

As she begins to analyze Migdalia's writing, Elena reminds herself that Migdalia, along with a few other students, is working on developing a more professional scientific register in her reports. She has on her desk a copy of the success criteria shared with students in Migdalia's group.

- Maintain an objective tone.

- Relay information efficiently and concisely. Try to combine related ideas into the same sentence to make it more efficient for your reader.

- Use connectors that make your logic clear to the reader.

As Elena has learned from Jason, it's best to start by considering whether or not the writing is effective, and noting what a student has done well. She notices that this write-up has a much more expert and objective tone than Migdalia's previous writing, and that the text is cohesive, showing skillful embedding of clauses within sentences (*First, they ask a scientific question that is not based on opinion, but can be tested*), as well as effective connections across sentences (*finally, in summation*). Elena is delighted to see how well Migdalia was able to make use of the success criteria.

In terms of the effectiveness in relation to the overall assignment (a report on how the scientific method could be used to test propulsion systems), however, Migdalia has not really written an effective report on that topic. What she has written is an effective procedure, which might be considered the Methods section of a science report.

Considering just this section that Migdalia has written and consulting the Performance Definitions, Elena concludes that Migdalia's writing most closely matches the characteristics of Level 3 writing. Elena makes note of Migdalia's growing, but not yet mastered, ability to fully match her writing to its purpose, which is consistent with what she sees in this language sample.

Setting Migdalia's Preliminary LLT

Because Elena has used the four lenses to analyze student language for so long, her application of the other lenses is simultaneous and almost instantaneous. It is clear to Elena that she will need to review with Migdalia the full set of genre expectations for a report in science, since Migdalia has written only the Procedure or Methods section of a full report. Looking closely at the section that Migdalia has written, Elena notes a significant change in the style, or *register*, of Migdalia's language in this report. In this case Migdalia has presented her ideas more objectively and more concisely than in the past.

When students are writing at such a proficient level, the task is more about fine-tuning language than about developing language, and there are often no large issues to be addressed. Instead, a number of small but important improvements can be made. Elena notes a vocabulary-related problem in the first sentence: scientists don't make investigations; they perform investigations. *Collocations* such as this one are learned through exposure, and this is an ideal opportunity to present this one to Migdalia. Elena also notes that, even in this highly effective piece, Migdalia could further tighten up her writing. The steps of the scientific method do not flow smoothly, but are interrupted by sentences in which Migdalia adds detail. This could be avoided by "tucking" the details into previous sentences, which would result in more concise writing and a less interrupted, more logical flow of ideas; for example, the idea expressed in sentence 6 might be embedded into sentence 4. Migdalia's writing sample is reproduced below, with the sentences numbered.

Steps to the Scientific Method

1. There are six steps of the Scientific Method that scientists use to help them make investigations.

2. First, they ask a scientific question that is not based on opinion, but can be tested.

3. The next step is to form a hypothesis that is a possible explanation to a scientific question that could be based on their observations.

4. The third step is to design an experiment by testing the factor in the scientific question.

5. In this case, the variables being tested are the type of propulsion system and how it's affecting fuel efficiency.

6. Scientists also have to keep the factors the same between the two things that they're testing.

7. Later, scientists collect data include the observations, data tables, and graphs.

8. Fifth, they analyze the results by comparing the data.

9. Finally, the last step is to draw a conclusion to see whether or not the hypothesis was supported.

10. In summation, the scientific method is a helpful tool for scientists to use in their experiments.

Combining the information in sentences 4, 5, and 6 would make the report more concise, as modeled here: *The third step is the design of a controlled experiment testing the effect of various propulsion systems on fuel efficiency.* Similarly, the information from sentences 7, 8, and 9 can be combined into one sentence: *After analyzing the data, which includes observations, data tables, and graphs, scientists conclude whether or not the data support the hypothesis.* Small changes like this make the writing more concise and avoid the simplistic, overworked "first, then, finally" connectors that students are taught at the early stages of writing, and on which they rely until they learn more complex, interesting, and concise ways of marking time and sequence. Elena is confident that Migdalia has sufficient command of varied syntactic forms to use them to make her writing more polished.

Elena notes one more change that would help Migdalia progress toward her personal writing goal. In several sentences, Migdalia uses a variety of verb forms (*The next step is to form a hypothesis; The third step is to design; the last step is to draw a conclusion; to see whether or not; and how it's affecting*) that could be replaced with the related noun forms of those verbs. The use of *nominalization* (a noun derived from a related verb or adjective) would help Migdalia maintain a more professional tone. Figure 2.6 shows examples of nominalization.

Informal Tone: Verb-based Form	Professional Tone: Nominalized Form
to form a hypothesis	*the formation of a hypothesis*
to design an experiment by testing the factor	*the design of an experiment testing the factor*
how it's affecting	*its effect on*

Figure 2.6 Examples of moving from verb-based to nominalized forms

This is one occasion when Elena thinks her colleagues might find her "just a bit too picky"; writing like Migdalia's is to be celebrated in the middle school grades! Indeed, Elena agrees with them on this point, but she also knows that Migdalia is driven to improve and deserves the chance to move beyond grade-level writing expectations. Migdalia will need excellent academic writing skills to succeed in college. Consequently, Elena develops LLTs focused on further development of an academic register and of Migdalia's ability to write coherently and concisely. Elena will discuss these LLTs with Migdalia during their writing conference.

Elena's preliminary LLTs for Migdalia include:

1. Use nominalization to maintain a more professional tone.

2. Combine sentences to maintain the clear, uninterrupted sequence of steps.

Migdalia's language assessment process is shown in Figure 2.7.

Lesson and Sampling	*Learning Objective*: Design and report on the use of the scientific method to test propulsion systems. *Sample*: An early draft of a science report, written as part of a "Write Like a Scientist" day assignment
Genre	Report

(continues)

(continued)

Success Criteria	• Maintain an objective tone. • Relay information efficiently and concisely. Try to combine related ideas into the same sentence to make it more efficient for your reader. • Use connectors that make your logic clear to the reader.
Language Sample	**Steps to the Scientific Method** There are six steps of the Scientific Method that scientists use to help them make investigations. First, they ask a scientific question that is not based on opinion, but can be tested. The next step is to form a hypothesis that is a possible explanation to a scientific question that could be based on their observations. The third step is to design an experiment by testing the factor in the scientific question. In this case, the variables being tested are the type of propulsion system and how it's affecting fuel efficiency. Scientists also have to keep the factors the same between the two things that they're testing. Later, scientists collect data include the observations, data tables and graphs. Fifth, they analyze the results by comparing the data. Finally, the last step is to draw a conclusion to see whether or not the hypothesis was supported In summation, the scientific method is a helpful tool for scientists to use in their experiments.
Analysis	*Strengths*: Migdalia shows a more expert and objective tone than in her previous writing. The text is cohesive, with some embedding of clauses within sentences as well as effective connections across sentences. *Genre and genre components*: She has written only one (Procedure) section of several required components of a report. *Text structure or organization*: Her report is not as concise as it should be, and the logical flow of ideas is interrupted by sentences with details that could have been inserted into surrounding sentences.

(continues)

(continued)

Analysis *(con't)*	*Grammatical forms*: The use of nominalization could help Migdalia maintain a consistently professional tone. *Vocabulary*: There is a collocation issue in the first sentence.
Initial, Teacher-derived LLTs	1. Use nominalization to maintain a more formal tone. 2. Combine sentences when able to maintain the clear, uninterrupted sequence of steps.
Formative Feedback Discussion	
Collaboratively Developed LLTs	
Tool to Collect Information	

Figure 2.7 Migdalia's language assessment process

Final Thoughts: Using Four Lenses to Set LLTs

In this chapter we've described the systematic use of four lenses to analyze language samples. Used together, these lenses highlight students' strengths and growing points with English. We have shown examples in which errors in punctuation and spelling—features too often marked in bright red ink as the only language elements for students to pay attention to—stand out as temptingly simple things to ask students to "fix." By resisting that urge in our examples, however, we hope to help teachers focus on improving students' ability to make meaning, and to do so in ways that suit the various contexts in which students will learn and work throughout their lives.

3

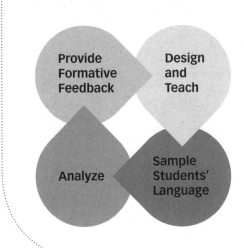

Provide Formative Feedback

Design and Teach

Analyze

Sample Students' Language

Involving Our Students in the Journey: Providing Formative Feedback

"'Assessment' comes from 'assidere' [Latin], which means 'to sit with'. Assessment is something we do with and for students."
—Margaret Heritage (2010a, p. 7)

The three examples discussed in the previous chapters outline clear success criteria for students and illustrate an important early step in engaging students in the process of language assessment for formative purposes. In this chapter, we'll discuss and show examples of the next critical step: provide formative feedback. Giving students feedback that is formative—that gives them the information and tools they need to improve their performance—does more than help improve their language skills. It brings them on board as active partners in their learning and helps them develop the meta-cognitive focus and skills essential to being effective learners.

We'll explain what effective formative feedback is and how teachers provide it to students. Then we'll put these concepts to work, rejoining the teachers as they meet with students Jorge, Kia, and Migdalia to provide formative language feedback, firm up their proposed LLTs, and begin to think about how they'll collect the next round of evidence of learning.

What Does Effective Formative Feedback Look Like?

Talking with students about their learning and progress is the most important step in formative assessment. Formative feedback has been called "the most powerful single moderator in the enhancement of achievement" (Hattie & Jaeger 1998). But what is the information that should be shared? What happens in those conversations that make them so powerful?

Not just any information about student performance qualifies as formative feedback. Here are the views of several formative assessment experts:

- "One of the most important roles in assessment is the provision of timely and informative feedback to students during instruction and learning . . ." (National Research Council 2001, p. 87).

- Formative feedback is "information communicated to the learner that is intended to modify his or her thinking or behavior for the purpose of improving learning" (Shute 2008).

- Formative feedback provided by teachers offers corrective advice to students in troubleshooting and self-correcting their work. This helps students take action to reduce the gap between their goals and their current production (Nicol & Macfarlane-Dick 2006, p. 208).

- At the same time, though, this information has to be used to inform the teaching and learning process. Feedback is formative if it leads to improved student learning (Tuttle 2009).

Simply returning graded papers to students does little to help them figure out how to improve. To provide formative feedback—information that supports students' "formation" as effective communicators of their ideas—a teacher needs to figure out what students need and how to provide it as they are in the process of learning, rather than simply estimating their effectiveness after the fact. Here are seven characteristics of effective formative feedback.

1. The feedback is timely, delivered when the student is learning, rather than after a product of student learning has been delivered for final, or summative, assessment.

2. The feedback is simple, specific, and brief, focusing clearly on just a few important elements.

3. The feedback opens a dialogue, rather than merely transmitting information.

4. The feedback is framed by clear criteria for what good performance looks like.

5. The feedback makes clear how current performance relates to good performance.

6. The feedback enables students to determine what to do to close the gap between current and good performance by providing corrective advice, not just information on strengths and weaknesses.

7. The feedback does not focus on grades, compare student performances, or discourage the learner.

Sources of Formative Feedback

Formative feedback can come from many sources. Teachers or peers can provide feedback to students. Students can reflect on their own work in the form of a self-assessment. As a point of departure, we offer an overview of the sources of formative feedback.

Teacher Feedback

Teachers constantly collect and communicate information about student performance, from grades on tests and assignments to verbal responses to student behavior. Nicol & Macfarlane-Dick (2006), as well as others noted, offer some specific strategies for turning that information into a tool that students can use to change their behaviors and improve their learning.

- Provide feedback on work in progress and increase opportunities for resubmission.

- Introduce two-stage assignments where feedback on Stage One helps improve Stage Two (Gibbs & Simpson 2004).

- Model strategies to close a performance gap in class.

- Provide action points along with the normal feedback comments.

- Involve groups of students in identifying their own action points in class after they have read the feedback on their assignments.

Peer Feedback

Students also gather information about academic performance, their own and that of others. Given the right opportunities, and appropriate training and support, peers become rich sources of formative feedback. Of course, teachers will need to create these opportunities (Nicol & Macfarlane-Dick 2006, p. 211). Suggested activities include:

- Asking students to read the feedback comments they have been given on an assignment and discuss these with peers, inviting the whole group to suggest strategies to improve performance as they progress in the assignment.

- Asking students to find one or two examples of feedback comments they found useful and to explain to their peers how these comments helped them better understand the material.

- Asking students to give each other descriptive feedback on their work before submission, using specific criteria.

- Asking students to discuss criteria and standards before beginning work on a group project.

Self Feedback

Structured self-reflection and self-assessment can help make students aware of areas where they can improve. The key here is structure, for few students are prepared to assess their progress on their own. Nicol and Macfarlane-Dick (2006) describe several ways of structuring self-assessment as part of a cycle of formative feedback.

- Allow students to request a particular focus for the feedback they would like when they hand in work.

- Ask students to identify strengths and weaknesses in their own work using preset criteria or rubrics before handing it in for teacher feedback.

- Have students reflect on their achievements and select work to compile as a portfolio.

- Ask students to reflect on achievement milestones before a task and on progress after a task (George & Cowan 1999).

Providing Formative Feedback to Jorge, Kia, and Migdalia

Let's return to the interactions between the teachers and students. Up to this point, the feedback the teachers have planned is based on their own analysis. Let's see how they widen the circle to include others in this important process.

Deeper learning is enhanced when formative assessment is used to: (1) make learning goals clear to students, (2) continuously monitor, provide feedback, and respond to students' learning progress, and (3) *involve students in self- and peer assessment.* (National Research Council 2012, p. 166, emphasis added).

Formative Feedback Conversation with Jorge

Elena has developed some preliminary ideas about LLTs for Jorge, based on her analysis of his written procedure for solving two-step equations. Before she begins to tell Jorge about her ideas, though, she will ask him for his ideas about the piece he wrote. She really wants to keep Jorge as an active, engaged partner, and she has taken time to understand his feelings and ideas about writing. She knows that Jorge did not enjoy writing in sixth grade; his papers came back with many errors marked in red and he did not understand how to fix them. Jorge is proud of knowing three languages and felt ashamed of all the errors. He has enjoyed Elena's approach to helping him analyze his writing, which has been to focus on getting his ideas across. Elena has assured him that just as he did not get to be a good soccer player or a good guitarist all at once, he does not need to worry about getting everything perfect all at once in his writing.

Elena begins, as planned, by asking Jorge what he thought of the piece he wrote on solving two-step equations. Jorge has a big grin and gestures excitedly when he tells her, "Writing about it helped me figure it out. I was confused before, but now I get it!" With his essay on the table in front of them, she asks him to tell her about the procedure one more time. She notes how frequently he points to examples on the board or scribbles an example on his paper. At various points, she stops him and asks, "But what if we were talking on the phone, and I couldn't see what you're pointing to? How would you explain what you mean?" When it seems to her that Jorge gets the point of this, she suggests that they find all the places in his written procedure where someone who was not in the same room would need more information. As they do this, it gives her an opportunity to help Jorge learn what happens in readers' minds when they hear "the": "They think that you're talking about something you've already told them about, and that can get pretty confusing." Following this, she shows Jorge the chart of genres and their components, and she asks him to color-code the various sections of his written procedure so they can see what might be missing and what might be "extra."

Jorge's LLT

Next, Elena and Jorge review the success criteria for this assignment, and Elena asks Jorge to name two criteria he thinks they should focus their attention on for the next procedure they will write in class.

1. Include the orientation, sequence, and outcome.

2. Provide enough detail so that each step is clear and easy for a reader to follow. Remember that your reader can't see anything but your words.

3. Don't distract the reader with unnecessary information.

4. Make sure the reader can tell when you move from one step to another.

5. Make the order of the steps clear.

Jorge identifies criteria 2, 3, and 4—one more than Elena had planned—but the addition of criterion 4 will provide an opportunity to address the improvements Jorge needs to make in his sentence formation, punctuation, and capitalization, so she endorses the plan. As students work together in Jorge's group, she will have them mark slashes on one another's papers wherever they see a period or capital letter, and then have the trio of students discuss whether those slashes do actually separate steps in the procedure. This should help her students understand the importance of placing these sentence markers correctly, and will embed her instruction about the correct forms and conventions for sentences into a meaning-based context.

Elena decides to pattern the LLTs after the success criteria, rather than to use the wording she had originally planned. The ideas are the same, and because Jorge's past experiences in writing have been so difficult for him, Elena wants to avoid the impression that his work will be judged by multiple, different sets of criteria.

Now that she is confident that Jorge has a better understanding of what is meant by criterion 2, she wants to bring other sources of feedback to bear on Jorge's writing. So, she suggests that Jorge plan to meet with two other students in a small group when the class starts writing the next procedure in math class. This group of three will share their papers and give one another specific feedback, using a tool that she will help them develop. This is discussed in more depth in Chapter 4. Figure 3.1 shows Jorge's language assessment process.

Lesson and Sampling	Grade 7 mathematics class, written procedure for solving two-step equations sampled from math journal. Part of a longer unit in which students explore additional equation types, working out and writing procedures for each.
Genre	Procedure
Success Criteria	• Provide enough detail so that each step is clear and easy for a reader to follow. Remember that your reader can't see anything but your words. • Don't distract the reader with unnecessary information. • Make sure the reader can tell when you move from one step to another. • Make the order of the steps clear.

(continues)

(continued)

Language Sample	Two. Step. Equation. Essay.
	In solving a two step equation problems the first step would be Isolating your variable. and some evidence would be having a variable next to the number. then you inverse the operation. and what happens to one side you do to the other side. and you get rid of the coeifficient the number with the variable. and when your done solving the problem you check your answer. and an example we did as a group was 3n–6=15 and the steps for solving this problem is you Box the number with the variable, then you Inverse of operation and the last step you do is divide. alsotheise problems are very easy to solve an sometimes hard to solve. and another example we did as a group was 5–x=17 and that problem was kind of hard to solve but the tutors showed us how to solve it step by step
Analysis	*Strengths*: It's clear that Jorge has learned some of the operations in the procedure (isolating a variable, using an inverse operation) and has used some transition words to show the sequence of mathematical operations.

Genre components: Jorge has used a brief orientation statement. There is evidence of an attempt to sequence steps. There is no clear closure. An unnecessary component has been included: a personal opinion, with a related example.

Text structure or organization: The text is not structured to suit its purpose of providing information in the absence of visual referents. The demarcation between steps is unclear after the initial steps.

Grammatical forms: Jorge may be attempting to use more varied language structures, but errors in punctuation and capitalization make this difficult to discern.

Vocabulary: Jorge has used several content-specific terms (*isolate*, *variable*, *coefficient*) accurately, and has used one (*inverse*) incorrectly as a verb. |

(continues)

(continued)

Initial, Teacher-derived LLTs	• Make your descriptions clear to readers who can't see your computations. Think carefully every time you use a pronoun (*it, that one, the other one*) and ask yourself whether the reader will know what you're referring to. • Remove any details that aren't part of the genre components for a procedure.
Formative Feedback Discussion	Jorge added one LLT to the teacher's list.
Collaboratively Developed LLTs	• Provide enough detail so that each step is clear and easy for a reader to follow. Remember that your reader can't see anything but your words. • Don't distract the reader with unnecessary information. • Make sure the reader can tell when you move from one step to another. (Check your sentence markers.)
Tool to Collect Information	

Figure 3.1 Jorge's language assessment process

Formative Feedback Conversation with Kia

As Jason prepares to meet with Kia, he reminds himself that Kia has not been very interested in writing, but now that she has become involved in social media she is motivated to make sure she looks good when she writes. He has in mind an LLT focused on prepositional phrases, but wants to hear Kia's thoughts about her needs before sharing his own ideas.

Jason begins his conversation with Kia by congratulating her on using the three new vocabulary words in her writing and on her use of the sentence frames, then asks her to tell him about the three ideas she listed. This gives him a chance to clarify Kia's confusion about the farmers and to clarify his own confusion about "come destroyed about." Kia responds that she wasn't sure the ideas she wrote down were the important ones from the article she read, and she didn't understand why the farmers destroyed things. As the conversation unfolds, Jason learns that the "farmers" Kia refers to are really plantation owners representing the slave states, who felt strongly that if the new government passed a law prohibiting slavery it would destroy their livelihood. Realizing the misperceptions Kia's partial understanding led to, Jason understands that Kia should have had more supports as she was reading—a fact he will remember next time—and proceeds to clarify the ideas Kia finds confusing.

Given their new, shared understanding of the ideas Kia was working to express, Jason and Kia will rewrite the sentences to clarify Kia's meaning. This will give Jason an opportunity to demonstrate the form of the prepositional phrase and to develop some additional models for Kia to use. Jason also realizes that Kia needs much more support for her writing, and he will develop additional sentence frames and graphic organizers that they will use together to organize her ideas into the relevant genre components.

Kia's LLT

Although Jason had planned to review the previous success criteria with Kia during this session, Jason realizes that the success criteria he's written are not appropriate for Kia at this point. The second criterion (*Include all the important ideas. Give enough detail so the reader understands what happened and why, but don't confuse your readers by giving information they don't need.*) will be out of Kia's reach unless he can better support her reading comprehension. Looking once again at the LLPs for social studies, he drafts new LLTs involving both Kia's reading and writing. They are designed to give Kia essential writing practice while also helping her develop a meta-cognitive focus and the practice of seeking assistance when she needs it, as well as to build her perseverance in reading.

1. I will write one sentence describing (explaining) each main idea in assigned social studies readings. I will add details in prepositional phrases.

2. I will circle parts of my reading that I don't understand.

3. If I don't understand an idea, I will ask a classmate or teacher to explain it.

Jason knows that this last target will be challenging for Kia, who is quite shy around her classmates, but he also knows that in a fast-paced classroom like Kevin's, Kia can fall behind quickly if she doesn't seek help when she needs it. He will talk with Kevin about checking in frequently with Kia, providing additional supports for her reading and making sure readings are discussed in small group sessions. When Jason meets with Kia, he will note what sorts of language structures she has circled and will use this information to guide his choices about what to teach next. Because Kia will need extensive support reading primary source documents, with their unfamiliar syntactic structures and formal register, he will work with Kevin to develop additional supports for Kia's reading.

In the next chapter you'll read about the tool Jason and Kia devise to help track her progress toward her new LLTs.

Kia's language assessment process is shown in Figure 3.2.

Lesson and Sampling	Grade 7 Sheltered Social Studies unit on the development of the U.S. Constitution, which will ultimately focus on the Argument genre. Early on, however, students are reading primary and secondary source documents about the Constitutional Convention and writing brief reports on their assigned readings. *Sample*: Report based on assigned reading.
Genre	Report
Success Criteria	• Summarize the important events and ideas. • Do not re-tell everything you read.
Language Sample	Piledafea, shermon become with the plan of the consititution. All of the people in the united states had to vote for a new consititution so that people and their slaves would have their natural rights. The meeting at phildaphe, the 9 states had to vote for a new consititoion. Then the farmers come destoryed about everyting of the government.
Analysis	*Strengths*: She has captured some ideas from the reading, has used three new vocabulary words, and has attempted new sentence structures. *Genre and genre components*: Not present. *Text structure or organization*: She has used sentence frames, linking ideas with "so that" to express purpose. *Grammatical forms*: She has used a sentence frame for sentence 2 to link clauses; she may have attempted prepositional phrases in sentences 1 and 3. *Vocabulary*: Several word choices are confusing.
Initial, Teacher-derived LLTs	Work on constructing prepositional phrases to add details within a sentence.

(continues)

(*continued*)

Formative Feedback Discussion	Clarification of ideas from reading assignment. Teacher realized that Kia needs much more reading support, and meta-cognition and classroom practices need to be built to help her access reading assistance when she needs it.
Collaboratively Developed LLTs	I will write one sentence describing (explaining) each main idea in assigned social studies readings. I will add details in prepositional phrases. I will circle parts of my reading that I don't understand. If I don't understand an idea, I will ask a classmate or teacher to explain it.
Tool to Collect Information	

Figure 3.2 Kia's language assessment process

Formative Feedback Conversation with Migdalia

Elena plans to focus attention on additional ways to help Migdalia make her writing more concise and professional in tone. She'll do this by having Migdalia work on embedding information into longer sentences, rather than using separate sentences, and using nominalization at times. She wants to focus intensely on what Migdalia has written, rather than starting off with her need to develop other sections of the report. She is confident that Migdalia will apply the new learning to those additional sections when she writes them.

Elena begins by asking Migdalia her opinion of her latest writing, and she is pleased when Migdalia recognizes that her report "sounds like a real report, and not a letter to my friends." Elena asks Migdalia to show her some specific changes she made that led to this change in register and congratulates her when Migdalia shows her some sentences in which she combined ideas concisely. She then asks Migdalia to examine the sentence that begins "The third step is to design . . ." and the two sentences that follow it. (See Chapter 2 for the sentence revisions described here.) Elena shares with Migdalia her reflection that the two sentences about the variables being tested and the need to keep variables constant seem to disrupt the orderly recount of steps in the procedure. Elena asks Migdalia to see whether she can embed all the information into one sentence to maintain the ordered sequence of steps without interruption. Next, she and Migdalia work on combining the ideas in sentences 7, 8, and 9, and they discuss the effect the changes make. Migdalia agrees with Elena that those changes make her writing seem more polished.

Elena has considered how to approach the concept of nominalization with Migdalia, to make sure it is focused on strengthening Migdalia's ability to tailor her writing to a specific context rather than introducing it as a decontextualized strategy. She asks Migdalia, "Is the important focus here on the actions scientists take, or is it on the process of scientific inquiry?" This is a very subtle distinction, one that a highly skilled writer would make, and one that would not be expected at the middle school level. Elena believes that this advanced writing is within Migdalia's reach, however, and wants to find a way to show her the change that results when verb forms are replaced with nominalizations. To make her point, Elena rewrites two of the sentences, as follows:

The next step is to form a hypothesis that is a possible explanation to a scientific question that could be based on their observations.

as

The next step is the formation of a hypothesis: a possible explanation that could be based on observations.

She rewrites

The third step is to design an experiment by testing the factor in the scientific question.

as

The third step is the design of an experiment testing the factor . . .

Together she and Migdalia discuss the difference these changes make. She asks Migdalia which set of sentences talks about the actions people take, and which set talks about the scientific process more as a thing in itself. Migdalia replies that the original sentences "still have the people in them, sort of like shadows" and that they are focused on the actions scientists take, but that the revised sentences do focus more on the scientific process rather than the actions. Together they examine a few well-written paragraphs from a scientific journal and experiment with changing the nominalizations back to verb forms, which helps to clarify the distinction even further. Elena stresses that both ways of expressing these ideas are correct, but that the revised sentences are more aligned with polished, professional writing. Elena and Migdalia work out a few more nominalizations to replace the "person doing something" structure of a few more sentences, and Elena asks Migdalia to see whether she can carry that new pattern through the rest of the paragraph. She pulls out the Genre Components chart to review with Migdalia what other sections still need to be written. Together they check the notebook of example reports and discuss the additional sections that need to be included in Migdalia's next draft.

Together Elena and Migdalia revise Elena's initial LLTs, and Elena asks Migdalia to try out the nominalization strategy when she writes the missing sections of the report. More specifically, she asks her to write a few sentences in both styles, and to discuss with her writing partner any differences they perceive in the effect of the two different styles.

Migdalia's New LLTs

1. Use nominalization to maintain the focus on the discussion of the method, not on the scientists or their actions.

2. Combine sentences when able to maintain the clear, uninterrupted sequence of steps.

Elena tells Migdalia that she will work on a tool that Migdalia and her writing partner can use to give one another feedback on their next draft of this report.

Migdalia's language assessment process is shown in Figure 3.3.

Lesson and Sampling	*Learning Objective*: Design and report on the use of the scientific method to test propulsion systems. *Sample*: An early draft of a science report, written as part of a "Write Like a Scientist" day assignment.
Genre	Report
Success Criteria	• Maintain an objective tone. • Relay information efficiently and concisely. Try to combine related ideas into the same sentence to make it more efficient for your reader. • Use connectors that make your logic clear to the reader.
Language Sample	**Steps to the Scientific Method** There are six steps of the Scientific Method that scientists use to help them make investigations. First, they ask a scientific question that is not based on opinion, but can be tested. The next step is to form a hypothesis that is a possible explanation to a scientific question that could be based on their observations. The third step is to design an experiment by testing the factor in the scientific question. In this case, the variables being tested are the type of propulsion system and how it's affecting fuel efficiency. Scientists also have to keep the factors the same between the two things that they're testing. Later, scientists collect data include the observations, data tables and graphs

(continues)

(*continued*)

Language Sample (*con't*)	Fifth, they analyze the results by comparing the data. Finally, the last step is to draw a conclusion to see whether or not the hypothesis was supported In summation, the scientific method is a helpful tool for scientists to use in their experiments.
Analysis	*Strengths*: Migdalia's report has a more expert and objective tone than previous writing; the text is cohesive, showing some embedding of clauses within sentences as well as effective connections across sentences. *Genre and genre components*: She has written only one (Procedure) section of several required components of a report. *Text structure or organization*: It is not as concise as it should be, and the logical flow of ideas is interrupted by sentences that add details that could have been inserted into surrounding sentences. *Grammatical forms*: The use of nominalization could help Migdalia to maintain a consistently professional tone. *Vocabulary*: There is a collocation issue in the first sentence.
Initial, Teacher-derived LLTs	• Use nominalization to maintain a formal tone. • Combine sentences when able to maintain the clear, uninterrupted sequence of steps.
Formative Feedback Discussion	Focused first on Migdalia's choices that led to increased concise style, then on how to tighten up topical control with nominalization.
Collaboratively Developed LLTs	• Use nominalization to maintain the focus on the discussion of the method, not on the scientists or their actions. • Combine sentences when able to maintain the clear, uninterrupted sequence of steps.
Tool to Collect Information	

Figure 3.3 Migdalia's language assessment process

Final Thoughts: **Using Effective Formative Feedback**

As exemplified in these scenarios, Jason and Elena have used their knowledge about effective formative feedback to do several things.

- They engaged their students in dialogue about their learning.

- They focused on increasing students' effectiveness in a few key elements of language rather than on a "laundry list" of errors.

- They provided on-the-spot instruction and clear ideas for moving forward.

Additionally, although this round of feedback was between one teacher and student, they have set in motion a plan for enhanced self-assessment for Kia, group analysis and feedback for Jorge, and partner analysis and feedback for Migdalia. In the next chapter we'll see the formative assessment tools they'll devise to gather evidence of new learning.

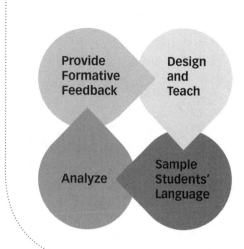

4

Staying on Course: Developing Tools to Gather Information About Student Progress

"For assessment to be 'formative' in terms of instruction, it must produce data that can inform teaching practice during its ongoing course."

—Fred Erickson
(2007, p. 189)

In this chapter we describe some tools that can help us monitor our students' progress toward their learning targets. Gathering helpful evidence at the right moments requires careful planning, but when we're engaging in the cyclic process of instruction and assessment the steps actually flow seamlessly. It is hard to imagine a teacher who does one step on Monday, the next one on Tuesday, and so on. Instead, formative assessment is woven into the instructional process. The only real distinction between planning instruction and planning information gathering is that we need to figure out how to keep track of what we notice and of the evidence we gather, often on the fly. The formative assessment tools described in this chapter are simply supports for our information gathering.

Given the wealth of information relayed in the previous chapters, we've chosen to separate this information in its own chapter so that readers can come back to it again and again as they plan instruction and make decisions about which tools to use or develop. As the narrative about teachers Kevin, Jason, and Elena and their students makes clear, the place to start planning formative assessment is right at the beginning of lesson or unit planning.

When formative assessment is part of early planning, teachers can design tools and strategies that do double duty, giving them a glimpse of students' developing content knowledge and language skill at the same time. Lesson-embedded formative assessment gives insight into the learning that is happening and can help us intervene as needed to shift the process for groups and individuals. Here are some comments from participating teachers of the FLARE project, on how formative assessment tools actually helped them to save time:

- It saves me time by allowing for quick feedback and in turn allows for flexible lesson planning.

- It gives me a method to provide immediate feedback in a short period of time, so I end up saving time.

This chapter describes a set of proven formative assessment tools and presents some tool templates—but with two caveats. First, these tools cannot replace the work of weaving language instruction into content lessons, gathering and interpreting evidence of language use, establishing language learning targets that are integrated into content learning, and giving students actionable information to help them move forward along their paths toward more effective expression of their ideas. That is, these powerful tools are part of the cycle that we have described in previous chapters and not a replacement for that cycle. These tools are best used after teachers have developed a good understanding of their students' language performance and have provided individualized feedback to direct and support their next steps. Our second caveat is this: Many sources provide detailed descriptions of how to build formative assessment tools, and we will not do that here. Instead, we will discuss three tools that will serve as models and are frequently used in busy classrooms. At the end of the chapter we will put these tools to work, returning to the narrative of teachers Jason, Kevin, and Elena and students Jorge, Kia, and Migdalia.

Building Tools to Assess Language for Formative Purposes

To get a good measure of students' progress, we need to pick the tool that makes sense. Just as a carpenter doesn't use a hammer to build everything, a teacher shouldn't use a checklist to monitor progress on every task. The process described next can help us decide what tool to use to yield the kind of data and the level of detail needed.

Step 1. Be Clear About What Kind of Data You Need

Picking the right tool to help us in our information-gathering begins with being clear about students' language learning targets and the learning opportunities that you have planned. Do we want to gather information about how a student is progressing in self-monitoring of new behaviors? Maybe a checklist would capture that information simply and quickly. Or maybe we need to keep track of how students are developing in terms of their self-assessed reading comprehension during a difficult reading assignment, in which case a rating scale might yield the information needed. (We might also choose to combine that with a check-list of actions to help students resolve their comprehension difficulties in the moment, to see which strategies students have used and found helpful.) Or perhaps we need to record a more fine-grained analysis of a student's developing skill with a particular language feature over a series of drafts, in which case we might create a rubric to capture that information. We might want some tools that students can use, and we might want some tools that only we will use. We might even want some tools to use with one or a small number of students, and then other tools for use with the entire class.

Whatever our purpose, we need to be sure that the tool will yield actionable data with which we can do something. The "formativity" of data (Erickson 2007)—its proximity to instruction, its relationship to an understood learning progression, and its link to a theory of action—is critical. Formative assessment involves not just assessing students more frequently; it means interpreting the evidence and using the information to take action during instruction.

Step 2. Consider the Options

Here are three frequently used and easily adapted tools, although once we have these in our kit, we may, like any good carpenter, want to develop others. However, these three can fill many of our needs.

Checklists

Checklists are quick and easy self-monitoring tools that help both students and teachers track ongoing progress toward developing new habits or using new resources consistently. Checklists can give students helpful reminders about what to focus on until they eventually internalize the steps of the particular task. Alone or in collaboration with students, we decide which questions to include, and then write questions that can be answered in a simple yes or no way. Here are some tips for creating effective checklists:

1. Identify only a small number of important elements related to the next stage or step in our student's learning.

2. List each item very simply, and keep the format consistent for all items.

3. If the checklist is for a procedure, list the steps in the order in which they should occur.

4. Include only items that can be answered yes or no.

Figure 4.4 (later in this chapter) shows the self-monitoring checklist that Jason and Kia developed to assist Kia in gathering information about her practice of new behaviors.

Rating Scales

When students are in the midst of developing new knowledge or skill, and attention is focused on their growing level of skill with particular language features, rating scales provide a simple way to capture rough estimates of where students are as they integrate and apply new knowledge. Rating scales do not need to have equivalent intervals or even the clearest criteria; rather, they're intended to give a quick and rough sketch of where the students are in relation to a learning objective. Having this information at hand can help us decide whether it's time to move to the next step in instruction or whether to provide refreshed, revised instruction for a few students or the entire class.

It's often helpful to construct a rating scale in collaboration with our students. Doing so can help make explicit the too-often hidden assumptions about what is important and what successful performance looks like. These are important lessons for all students, but they are especially important for students who are new to the culture and expectations of American classrooms. Here are some tips for creating effective rating scales.

1. Identify a small number of items to rate.

2. State those items clearly and simply, using language comprehensible to all students, and include visual supports as needed.

3. Since these are rough estimates of progress toward a target, decide how many "levels" can be rated reasonably and easily. Are three enough for the purpose, or do you need more? Can this quick tracking of student progress really be sorted into five levels, or is that too many?

Figure 4.2 (later in this chapter) shows the rating scale Elena developed to help Jorge and his writing group prepare for and gather information during their peer feedback conversations.

Rubrics

Sometimes we want a more fine-grained analysis of students' progress toward a goal, and a rubric is the most useful tool in a situation like this. Many students are familiar with rubrics because they are often used in grading, and students can benefit greatly from examining and practicing with the scoring rubrics that will be applied eventually to their finished work. Using the same rubric that a teacher uses—or even better, developing one together with the teacher—can help students become aware of what good performance looks like and what elements are considered most important. Students' application of rubrics to their own work can enhance their meta-cognitive focus and their involvement in their own learning. Scoring rubrics define and clearly show specific characteristics that students can use as a guide for improvement and offer a known scale of performance, along which students can measure their own progress.

The same rubric could serve dual purposes. What distinguishes rubrics used for formative purposes from those used for grading is simply who uses them and for what purposes.

When students use them to keep track of their movement over time toward a goal, they are formative. When teachers or students use them to compare a final product against a set of performance criteria, they are summative, grading rubrics. Here are some tips for creating effective scoring rubrics:

- Make sure the criteria that are well understood and clearly stated.

- Focus on only the most important elements.

- Create enough levels or intervals to reflect the level of detail needed, but also the level of differentiation that can honestly be obtained in the context.

- Make sure they're written in a language students can use.

Figure 4.6 (later in this chapter) shows the rubric that Elena developed for Migdalia and her writing partner.

These three examples demonstrate how even very simply constructed tools can support our evidence gathering. The key is in choosing the correct type of tool for the task. Figure 4.1 summarizes the information about these three tool types.

Tool	Useful for . . .	For students	For teachers
Checklist Are my students becoming more consistent in . . .?	Recording, in a simple yes/no format, the inclusion of new behaviors or other elements students are working to integrate.	Helps students remember and learn the steps in a new process or new behaviors to practice.	Captures information quickly and easily; can be used easily by students.
Rating Scale "How well (roughly) are they doing?"	Getting an informal, continuum-based rating of elements considered important in the lesson or task.	Helps students rate their own comprehension of new material or their comfort with new practices. Focuses students' attention on meta-cognitive aspects and personal accountability for learning.	Quickly captures an informal rating of student's movement toward a goal.

(*continues*)

(*continued*)

| Rubric "What level are they at in their mastery of this?" | More carefully evaluating the quality of specific components of student work and deciding which level of performance best describes the work.
• Requires clearly specified criteria for each level of performance.
• Intervals/levels should be equivalent in range. | Involves students in judging their own mastery.
Helps develop meta-cognitive stance and skill.
Makes explicit what elements are important and what successful performance "looks like." | Assesses student movement toward criteria that will be used later to make a summative assessment of their performance. |

Figure 4.1 Choosing the correct type of tool for a task

Step 3. Pilot the Tool

Once we've built a tool for checking students' progress, we need to try it out to see how well it will work. If students will be using the tools, they should also have an opportunity to pilot them. Here are some questions to consider.

1. What did this tool tell me about whether my students are meeting instructional language goals or language learning targets?

2. Did it provide actionable information?

3. What levels of performance did I see? Did the levels or intervals I constructed relate well enough to my purpose?

With a piloted and revised tool in hand, we're ready to gather evidence of incremental changes in student performance at key points as lessons progress. We'll return to our seventh-grade classroom to see how Jason and Elena incorporate formative assessment tools into their work with Jorge, Kia, and Migdalia.

Creating Tools for the Three Students

Jorge's Language Assessment Tool

Jorge's LLTs are focused on helping him develop his skill in describing ideas and abstract entities without physical referents. Jorge is in a writing group with three other students who are working toward similar LLTs. One of the three students also has, like Jorge, difficulties with the *sentence signals* of periods and capital letters. Elena developed a rating scale, shown in

Figure 4.2, that all three will use to rate one another's papers before sharing their feedback with each other. The rating scale will serve as an information-gathering tool for them, to support their discussion as they reflect together on one another's writing.

At the top of the rating scale is a brief set of instructions for its use, which she reviews with the four students in the group. Marshaling the power of a group to critique one another's writing is an effective strategy if the group is well matched and able to function as peers without being overshadowed by one or two members. Elena's experience with her students makes her confident that this group will function well, but she will monitor their actions and their effectiveness.

Using this rating scale:				
• Use your partner's paper for this exercise. • First, put a slash mark wherever you see a period or capital letter—these are the "sentence signals" marking that a new step is being introduced. Fill out the first question on the rating scale. • Second, remember that you cannot see anything besides the words on the page. Fill out the second question on the rating scale. • Last, circle any information that does not seem to explain the procedure. Fill out the third question on the rating scale. • Be ready to explain your ratings to your writing partners and show them the examples that support your decisions.				
Do the sentence signals mark the change from one step to another?	Yes, always.	Most of the time.	Some of the time.	Not at all.
How many steps in the procedure you're reading can you understand— without looking at anything else?	I can understand all of the steps the way they're written.	I can understand most of the steps the way they're written.	I can understand only a few of the steps the way they're written.	I can't understand any of the steps the way they're written.
Is there unnecessary information?	No. Everything written belongs in a procedure.	Yes, some. There are a few things that don't belong in a procedure.	Yes, a lot. There are lots of things that don't belong in a procedure.	There are so many things that don't belong that it's very confusing to read.

Figure 4.2 Jorge's peer rating scale

Figure 4.3 shows Jorge's language assessment process.

Lesson and Sampling	Grade 7 math class, written procedure for solving two-step equations sampled from math journal. Part of a longer unit in which students explore additional equation types, working out and writing procedures for each.
Genre	Procedure
Success Criteria	• Provide enough detail so that each step is clear and easy for a reader to follow. Remember that your reader can't see anything but your words. • Don't distract the reader with unnecessary information. • Make sure the reader can tell when you move from one step to another. • Make the order of the steps clear.
Language Sample	**Two. Step. Equation. Essay.** In solving a two step equation problems the first step would be Isolating your variable. and some evidence would be having a variable next to the number. then you inverse the operation. and what happens to one side you do to the other side. and you get rid of the coeifficient the number with the variable. and when your done solving the problem you check your answer. and an example we did as a group was 3n−6=15 and the steps for solving this problem is you Box the number with the variable, then you Inverse of operation and the last step you do is divide. alsotheise problems are very easy to solve an sometimes hard to solve. and another example we did as a group was 5−x=17 and that problem was kind of hard to solve but the tutors showed us how to solve it step by step
Analysis	*Strengths*: It's clear that Jorge has learned some of the operations in the procedure (isolating a variable, using an inverse operation) and has used some transition words to show the sequence of mathematical operations.

(*continues*)

(*continued*)

Analysis (*con't*)	*Genre components*: Jorge has used a brief orientation statement. There is evidence of an attempt to sequence steps. There is no clear closure. An unnecessary component has been included: a personal opinion, with a related example. *Text structure or organization*: The text is not structured to suit its purpose of providing information in the absence of visual referents. The demarcation between steps is unclear after the initial steps. *Grammatical forms*: Jorge may be attempting to use more varied language structures, but errors in punctuation and capitalization make this difficult to discern. *Vocabulary*: Jorge has used several content-specific terms (*isolate*, *variable*, *coefficient*) accurately and has used one term (*inverse*) incorrectly as a verb.
Initial, Teacher-derived LLTs	1. Make your descriptions clear to readers who can't see your computations. Think carefully every time you use a pronoun (*it*, *that one*, *the other one*) and ask yourself whether the reader will know what you're referring to. 2. Remove any details that aren't part of the genre components for a procedure.
Formative Feedback Discussion	Jorge added one LLT to teacher's list.
Collaboratively Developed LLTs	• Provide enough detail so that each step is clear and easy for a reader to follow. Remember that your reader can't see anything but your words. • Don't distract the reader with unnecessary information. • Make sure the reader can tell when you move from one step to another. (Check your sentence markers.)
Tool to Collect Information	Peer rating scale

Figure 4.3 Jorge's language assessment process

Kia's Language Assessment Tool

Because Kia is in the early stages of developing strategies and habits to support her reading comprehension, Jason decides to use a simple yes/no checklist to gather information about Kia's progress in building these habits into her daily work. He and Kia worked together on the wording, and Jason is confident that Kia understands the checklist. The checklist presented in Figure 4.4 will help Kia collect and keep track of the information every day. When Kia and Jason discuss this record of Kia's self-monitoring, they will look back over the checklists for each day, noting any changes and discussing relevant factors that may have made these actions easier for Kia on some days than others.

Did I …?	Yes	No
Write one sentence describing each main idea?		
Put the details into prepositional phrases?		
Circle any parts of the reading that were confusing?		
Ask a classmate or teacher to explain an idea?		
Did anything make this easier or harder to do today?		

Figure 4.4 Kia's self-monitoring checklist

Figure 4.5 shows Kia's language assessment process.

Lesson and Sampling	Grade 7 Sheltered Social Studies unit on the development of the U.S. Constitution, which will ultimately focus on the Argument genre. Early on, however, students are reading primary and secondary source documents about the Constitutional Convention and writing brief reports on their assigned readings. Sample: Report based on assigned reading.
Genre	Report
Success Criteria	• Summarize the important events and ideas. • Do not retell everything you read.

(continues)

(continued)

Language Sample	Piledafea, shermon become with the plan of the consititution.
	All of the people in the united states had to vote for a new consititution so that people and their slaves would have their natural rights.
	The meeting at phildaphe, the 9 states had to vote for a new consititoion. Then the farmers come destoryed about everyting of the government
Analysis	*Strengths*: Kia has captured some ideas from the reading, has used three new vocabulary words, and has attempted new sentence structures.
	Genre and genre components: Not present
	Text structure or organization: She has used sentence frames, linking ideas with "so that" to express purpose.
	Grammatical forms: She has used sentence frames for sentence 2 to link clauses; she may have attempted using prepositional phrases in sentences 1 and 3.
	Vocabulary: Several word choices are confusing.
Initial, Teacher-derived LLTs	Work on constructing prepositional phrases to add details within a sentence.
Formative Feedback Discussion	Clarification of ideas from reading assignment. Teacher realized that Kia needs much more reading support, and to build meta-cognition and classroom practices to help her access reading assistance when she needs it.
Collaboratively Developed LLTs	• I will write one sentence describing (explaining) each main idea in assigned social studies readings. I will add details in prepositional phrases. • I will circle parts of my reading that I don't understand. • If I don't understand an idea, I will ask a classmate or teacher to explain it.
Tool to Collect Information	Self-monitoring checklist to track progress in developing new learning practices

Figure 4.5 Kia's language assessment process

Migdalia's Language Assessment Tool

Migdalia is refining her writing practice toward clearly defined goals, and her LLTs require a fine-grained focus on conciseness and cohesion. Elena will work with Migdalia and her writing partner on these elements, which are beyond the current reach and relevance of Migdalia's classmates. Because Elena will not meet with this peer feedback group often, she wants a tool to help her collect and keep track of this writing pair's movement toward their goals. She will use this collection of information when she meets with them. Elena knows that a rubric will provide the level of detail that she desires, and she developed the one shown in Figure 4.6.

Rubric for Science Report: Using the Scientific Method to Test Propulsion Systems	Evidence		
	1	2	3
Conveying sequence clearly and skillfully	Sequence is unclear, or some steps are missing.	Sequence is clear, and uses *first*, *second*, *third*, or *first*, *next*, and *finally* type of connectors.	Sequence is clear, and information about sequence is embedded into complex sentences: *After analyzing the data . . . scientists conclude*
Writing concisely	Sentences are not correctly written: there are run-on sentences or incomplete sentences.	Each sentence is correctly formed and has one main idea.	Each sentence contains two or three important ideas.
Control of topic	Topic is unclear.	Topic is clear, but not all sentences are focused on the topic.	Topic is clear, and all sentences are focused on the topic.

(continues)

(*continued*)

Nominalization	No nominalizations are used.	Nominalizations are used and are correctly formed.	Nominalizations are correctly formed and used for topical control.

Figure 4.6 Migdalia's peer assessment and feedback rubric

You can see Migdalia's language assessment process in Figure 4.7.

Lesson and Sampling	*Learning objective*: Design and report on the use of the scientific method to test propulsion systems. *Sample*: an early draft of a science report, written as part of a "Write Like a Scientist" day assignment.
Genre	Report
Success Criteria	• Maintain an objective tone. • Relay information efficiently and concisely. Try to combine related ideas into the same sentence to make it more efficient for your reader. • Use connectors that make your logic clear to the reader.
Language Sample	**Steps to the Scientific Method** There are six steps of the Scientific Method that scientists use to help them make investigations. First, they ask a scientific question that is not based on opinion, but can be tested. The next step is to form a hypothesis that is a possible explanation to a scientific question that could be based on their observations. The third step is to design an experiment by testing the factor in the scientific question. In this case, the variables being tested are the type of propulsion system and how it's affecting fuel efficiency. Scientists also have to keep the factors the same between the two things that they're testing. Later, scientists collect data include the observations, data tables and graphs. Fifth, they analyze the results by comparing the data. Finally, the last step is to draw a conclusion to see whether or not the hypothesis was supported In summation, the scientific method is a helpful tool for scientists to use in their experiments.

(*continues*)

(*continued*)

Analysis	*Strengths*: Migdalia's report has a more expert and objective tone than previous writing; the text is cohesive, showing some embedding of clauses within sentences as well as effective connections across sentences. *Genre and genre components*: She has written only one (Procedure) section of several required components of a report. *Text structure or organization*: It is not as concise as it should be, and the logical flow of ideas is interrupted by sentences that add details that could have been inserted into surrounding sentences. *Grammatical forms*: The use of nominalization could help. Migdalia maintains a consistently professional tone. *Vocabulary*: There is a collocation issue in the first sentence.
Initial, Teacher-derived LLTs	• Use nominalization to maintain a more formal tone. • Combine sentences when able to maintain the clear, uninterrupted sequence of steps.
Formative Feedback Discussion	Focused first on Migdalia's choices that led to increased concise style, then on how to tighten up topical control with nominalization.
Collaboratively Developed LLTs	• Use nominalization to maintain the focus on the discussion of the method, not on the scientists or their actions. • Combine sentences when able to maintain the clear, uninterrupted sequence of steps.
Tool to Collect Information	Peer assessment and feedback rubric focused on conciseness and topical control.

Figure 4.7 Migdalia's language assessment process

Final Thoughts: Building a Repertoire of Tools to Assess Language for Formative Purposes

The choice of a tool depends on the type of evidence we need to gather, which is in turn guided by our plan of action. The tools do not replace any step of the cycle. Rather, they support teachers—and students—in gathering and keeping track of a multitude of information in busy classrooms.

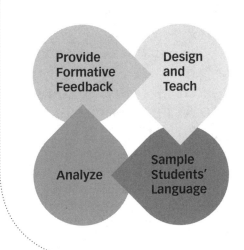

Provide Formative Feedback

Design and Teach

Analyze

Sample Students' Language

5

The Formative Assessment Cycle in Practice

We've shown the ways in which a focus on the formative assessment process fits into and enriches the daily practice of teachers and students. In this chapter we share some reflections—both the benefits and challenges—of teachers who have worked to incorporate formative assessment into their busy teaching schedules. This chapter covers the following key areas:

- Implementing a language-focused formative assessment model
- Changing ideas to change practice
- Putting it all together and getting back to students

Implementing a Language-focused Formative Assessment Model

Nationally, educators, policymakers, and researchers have argued for a more expansive view of assessment to include not only summative, but also benchmark and formative assessment (Redfield, Roeber, & Stiggins 2008). This balanced assessment system approach can be seen specifically in one of the two federal Race to the Top assessment grants, SBAC (www .smarterbalanced.org). Many researchers strongly support the use and value of formative or classroom assessment by teachers (e.g., Black & Wiliam 1998; Heritage 2010a, 2013; Popham 1995; Shepherd 2006; Stiggins 2005; Wiliam 2012).

Formative assessment has been the focus of a substantial amount of writing and some education research, and there is the beginning of consensus about what works. Across content areas, we now believe that a formative assessment process will be effective to the extent that it does the following:

- Is an ongoing, classroom-based process that is embedded in instruction

- Focuses students on learning goals

- Provides examples of good work

- Identifies students' current skills and abilities

- Builds on students' strengths, highlights students' gaps in learning goals, and provides methods to address gaps

- Focuses on learning targets that are coherent with external standards

- Is dynamic enough to accommodate classroom realities (e.g., easily accomplished, adjustable for disruptions, adjusts to student heterogeneity), yet is consistent in methods of data collection, interpretation, and reporting

- Incorporates a rigorous, sustained professional development program for teachers.

This is good news. We know what to work toward. Of course, there is still substantial work to do. Knowing what an ideal process should include is an important step. Using that knowledge to build models that are effective and workable in elementary and secondary educational contexts will take additional work in research and development. Additionally, we need to turn our attention to models that address the unique learning needs of ELLs and of the educators who support English learners, and that work is only beginning (McKay 2005).

Our five-year project on the assessment of language for formative purposes has led to this book, which provides a set of processes, guidelines, and analytic lenses to help teachers integrate content learning with attention to language. Using the formative assessment cycle, teachers can quickly and easily gather samples of student language, develop supports for their information gathering, and analyze student language to develop language-specific formative feedback to share with students. Our hope is that this cycle helps teachers understand that formative assessment is a process, not another type of test. We hope teachers will integrate formative assessment practices into their teaching practice.

Changing Ideas and Changing Practice

The concepts foundational to formative assessment are relatively simple and straightforward, and teachers can quickly learn and begin to integrate elements of formative assessment into their practice. Over time, with training and experience, teachers weave formative assessment seamlessly into their instruction as they develop an increasingly reflective, inquiry-based approach to instruction. Our experience has shown us, however, that teacher understanding alone is not sufficient. In at least one of the schools in which we piloted this project, teachers were required to provide grades for all student work—including the language samples gathered for formative assessment. This experience highlights the importance of administrative policy in supporting effective formative assessment. In the schools where principals were involved in the development and implementation of the formative assessment program, we saw positive results. In schools where principals were not involved, we saw challenges. A school's culture and leadership can support or sabotage implementation of the process. If district and school participants hold different perspectives on academic language or on formative assessment, getting all teachers and administrators on the same page regarding this critical construct is daunting. Teachers don't teach in a vacuum; administrative support, including shared understanding of new ways of working, is important to the success of a formative assessment initiative.

We also noted the importance of organizational structures that enabled teachers to work collaboratively and share information on the formative assessment tools they use and create. Some of the specific components are easy to put into use, but the change to the inquiry-based approach to teaching that is the basis of formative assessment needs time, support, and dedication. Book discussion groups, professional learning communities, and coaching can help teachers develop a deeper understanding of formative assessment practice. Teachers working together on grade-level teams or on curriculum teams can identify key points during instructional units where formative assessment strategies can be built into lessons to help teachers assess the effects of instruction up to that point and plan modifications as needed.

Some states and districts have developed systematic approaches to professional development that have resulted in sustained growth and skilled implementation of forative assessment. One excellent example, described on the Michigan Department of Education website (www.michigan.gov/mde), is the Formative Assessment for Michigan Educators initiative, known as the FAME project. The processes and resources they've developed (Michigan Department of Education 2010) can be helpful to districts planning a systematic approach to implementation. A school or district official that chooses to adopt a system to assess language for formative purposes without devoting resources to its training and implementation may meet with limited success, at best. We join others in the desire to understand more about "teacher uptake" of and success in using the formative assessment process.

Final Thoughts: Putting It All Together and Getting Back to the Students

During the years of working in school districts, we found that the use of appropriate, classroom-based, language assessment does change classroom practice. By helping teachers identify and focus on the language that will make a difference in their students' learning, teachers and students are supported in taking the next steps toward academic success.

Behind each of the teachers interviewed as part of our work stand many ELLs, all of whom are faced with doing twice the work of their English-fluent peers. Some are new to the country and culture, many are new to the expectations and practices of schools in the United States, but every one of them faces the double challenge of learning a new language and learning in the new language. The goal of the process outlined in this book is to help students and teachers understand what next steps to take to move forward toward success. It has great potential to support student learning; however, without substantial support for students, teachers, and principals, that potential will be greatly limited. This is a risk that we, and our ELLs, cannot afford.

About FLARE: Formative Language Assessment Records for English Language Learners

This book grew out of five years spent working on the Formative Language Assessment Records for English Language Learners (FLARE) project, a project funded by the Carnegie Corporation of New York. In the FLARE project, we collaborated with middle school and high school teachers in three school districts (Chicago Public Schools, Illinois; Charlotte-Mecklenburg Public Schools, North Carolina; and Garden Grove Unified School District, California) to develop practices to assess ELLs' language for formative purposes in secondary classrooms. The project brought together research on learning progressions with the procedures, tools, and insights of the many teachers with whom we've worked. What emerged from that project was a language-focused formative assessment model.

The FLARE project created this model by developing detailed language learning progressions (LLPs) that offer fine-grained analysis of student language performance and possible next steps, as well as formative assessment tools that focus on the language learning needs of ELLs. FLARE's LLPs are based on a review of research on academic language literacy development and an examination of available state content standards, English language development standards, and national college readiness standards. Integrating theories of how language learning unfolds with knowledge about the language requirements in school, the FLARE LLPs map a path for ELLs' development of academic language and academic literacy in middle and high school English language arts, mathematics, science and social studies.

FLARE's formative assessment process uses language learning progressions (LLPs) to establish instructional goals and objectives based on the language learning progressions, and, in turn, the process suggests teacher-friendly formative assessment tools that can be used to gather information about student progress and provide formative feedback to students and teachers based the analysis of the data gathered. The assessment process generates feedback about what ELLs need to learn next to inform teaching and learning.

Over three years, we piloted FLARE in the three school districts mentioned earlier. Again and again, we have found that the use of appropriate, classroom-based language assessment to monitor student progress in developing academic English in middle and high school grades changes classroom practices. It helps teachers identify and articulate the academic language of their core subject matter as separate from, yet essential to, content knowledge and skills. Simply put, the process helps ESL and bilingual teachers identify and focus on the language that will make a difference in their students' learning.

Between 2009 and 2011 the FLARE project team administered evaluative surveys and conducted focus groups in each of three participating school districts. Both survey and focus group questions asked about teachers' understanding of formative assessment, use of formative assessment materials, understanding of academic language literacy, and the challenges and benefits of integrating formative assessment into classroom practice. We found that teachers were able to use the process effectively, but at the same time we became aware of how such a shift in focus requires ongoing professional development and experimentation.

Responses from the teacher surveys and focus groups highlighted teachers' understanding of formative assessment in the participating school districts. Generally, teachers identified with our understanding of formative language assessment as a process that uses language learning progressions to help identify students' next steps in language development. Thus, FLARE was effective in countering the prevailing focus on assessment *of* learning, and moving teachers to an understanding of formative assessment as assessment *for* learning.

However, teacher responses also highlighted that teacher understanding alone is not sufficient. In at least one school, teachers were required to provide grades for all student work—including the language samples gathered for formative assessment, thus negating the purpose. Formative assessment is not about grading; it is about monitoring progress and adjusting instruction so that, by the time grades are due, students have received the assistance and support that will help them improve. Teachers highlighted the importance of administrative policy in supporting effective formative assessment. We don't teach in a vacuum; administrative support, including shared understanding of new ways of working, is important to the success of a formative assessment initiative.

As might be expected, some teachers found the use of formative assessment and the availability of the FLARE LLPs liberating, and others found it overwhelming. In two districts, where many teachers had 25 or more students in each of their classes, some found differentiation of instruction for ELLs and the use of the tools and LLPs laudable but unrealistic. Yet others from the same districts found the tools and progression helpful. Several teachers remarked that the process actually *saves* time, by helping them hone in quickly on students' specific needs. Certainly, training and familiarity with the process helped, and teaching load had a substantial impact, but we join others in the desire to understand more about "teacher uptake" of formative assessment as a process.

In launching the FLARE project, our hope was that the implementation of a systematic approach to assessing language for formative purposes would improve teacher practice in supporting ELLs. According to research, including an eight-year British study, ELLs taught in classrooms where teachers used formative assessment demonstrated significantly higher levels of English language proficiency. At least one study has shown that formative assessment is "particularly effective for students in narrowing the gap between low and high achievers while raising overall achievement" (Ross 2005). We collected, from teachers, evidence of how language assessment for formative purposes had changed their practice, and of teachers' beliefs about the potential of the process. For example, one teacher indicated that she began using the FLARE tools to better understand students' current academic language literacy and create more challenging materials. Another indicated that he began using tools more effectively. In both cases, these teachers became able to increase ELLs' meaningful engagement and their opportunities to learn.

Our hope in writing this book is that teachers will experiment with the processes and lenses we have distilled, and then share their successes and questions with colleagues. Language assessment for formative purposes is a new process, one that is deserving of all our attention and creativity. We hope that the information in this book will help teachers use the process effectively to support student learning.

GLOSSARY

Academic content standards
Statements that define what students are expected to know and be able to do to attain competency in challenging subject matter associated with schooling, such as state mathematics standards

Academic language
The vocabulary, grammatical structures, and discourse required in learning the academic content of school subjects; aspects of language strongly associated with literacy development and achievement

Cohesion
A feature of academic language at the discourse level involving the grammatical and lexical elements within and across sentences that hold text together to give it meaning

Collocations
Words or phrases that naturally co-occur with each other, (e.g., "peanut butter and jelly" or "a strong resemblance")

Discourse
Extended, connected oral or written language that may include detailed explanations, descriptions, and propositions

English Language Learners (ELLs)
Linguistically and culturally diverse students who have been identified through reliable and valid assessment as having levels of English language proficiency that preclude them from accessing, processing, and acquiring unmodified grade-level content in English, and thereby qualify for language support services

FLARE (Formative Language Assessment Records for English Language Learners)
A program, funded by the Carnegie Corporation of New York, for developing language learning progressions based on the strands of model performance indicators of the English language proficiency and college readiness standards, as the basis for creating and validating a formative, classroom assessment system in secondary settings

Formative assessment
A process used by teachers, and students and teachers, during instruction that provides feedback to adjust ongoing teaching and learning to improve students' educational outcomes

Formative feedback
Information communicated to the learner that is intended to modify his or her thinking or behavior to improve learning

Formative language assessment
An ongoing assessment process that provides students and teachers with in-the-moment feedback on progress toward linguistic instructional goals

Functional approach to language
A way of analyzing language in terms of its purposes, or functions, as opposed solely to analyzing its forms or correctness

General vocabulary
Words or phrases used in a variety of contexts inside and out of school (e.g., *tall*, *book*, *eat*)

Genres
In the context of language learning and assessment, refers to the ways we organize ideas for presentation to others, not to the categories of literature in English language arts classes

Language assessment for formative purposes
A lesson-embedded process for assessing the efficacy of students' language and interacting with students to support and guide the next steps in learning

Language function
How language learners process and use language to communicate in a variety of contexts and situations; the purpose for oral and written language use that also guides its structures

Language Learning Targets (LLTs)
Derived from the language learning progressions; the identified focus for proximal learning or "next steps"

Language Learning Progressions (LLPs)
Sequenced steps in academic English language development intended to support classroom instruction and framed by the four linguistic components: (1) text structure, (2) language functions, (3) language forms and conventions, and (4) vocabulary usage

Nominalization
The use of a noun derived from a verb or adjective (e.g., *erode-erosion*, *strong-strength*)

Register
Types of words and of syntactic and clausal structure that fit a specific context

Specific vocabulary
Academic terms or phrases used in school settings across the content areas of English language arts, mathematics, science, and social studies

Student self-assessment
Students' evaluation of their own progress and proficiency by reviewing their work to determine what they have learned and what areas of confusion still exist

Success criteria
Clear statements or examples that define effective performance

Summative assessment
An occasional (often annual) assessment that provides parents, educators, and policymakers with information about students' attainment of standard(s) or progress toward learning objectives

Technical vocabulary
Terminology associated with topics within the content areas of English language arts, mathematics, science, and social studies

Text structure
Describes how messages are communicated in subject areas; refers to the organizational techniques used to express ideas through language

Vocabulary usage
The type of vocabulary a student at a particular level should be able to comprehend or use appropriately

REFERENCES

Abedi, J. (Ed.). 2007. *English Language Proficiency Assessment in the Nation: Current Status and Future Practice.* Davis, CA: University of California, Davis School of Education.

Bailey, A. L. 2007. *The Language Demands of School: Putting Academic English to the Test.* New Haven, CT: Yale University Press.

Bailey, A. L., & Heritage, M. 2008. *Formative Assessment for Literacy, Grades K–6: Building Reading and Academic Language Skills Across the Curriculum.* Thousand Oaks, CA: Corwin/Sage Press.

Black, P., & Wiliam, D. 1998. "Assessment and Classroom Learning." *Assessment in Education: Principles, Policy and Practice, 5* (1), 7–74.

Bransford, J. D., Brown, A. L., & Cocking, R. R. 2000. *How People Learn.* Washington, DC: National Academy Press.

Brookhart, S. M. 2003. "Developing Measurement Theory for Classroom Assessment Purposes and Uses." *Educational Measurement Issues and Practices, 22* (4), 5–12.

Bunch, G. 2013. "Pedagogical Language Knowledge: Preparing Mainstream Teachers for English Learners in the New Standards Era." *Review of Research in Education.* March 2013, Vol. 37, 298–341.

Castro, M., Cook, H. G., & White, P. 2009 (Sept.). *Focus on Formative Assessment.* Retrieved from http://wida.us/resources#focus.

Chappuis, J., Stiggins, R., Chappuis, S., & Arter, J. 2011. *Classroom Assessment for Student Learning: Doing It Right—Using It Well.* Boston: Pearson Education.

Cook, H. G., & MacDonald, R. 2014. *Reference Performance Level Descriptors: Outcome of a National Working Session on Defining an "English Proficient" Performance Standard.* Washington, DC: Council of Chief State School Officers. Retrieved from www .sscco.org/Resources/Publications/Reference_Performance_Level_Descriptors .html.

Council of Chief State School Officers (CCSSO). 2012. *Distinguishing Formative Assessment from Other Educational Assessment Labels.* Washington, DC: Council of Chief State School Officers.

Derewianka, B. 1990. *Exploring How Texts Work.* Roselle, NSW, Australia: Primary Teaching Association.

Erickson, F. 2007. Chapter 8. "Some Thoughts on 'Proximal' Formative Assessment of Student Learning." *Yearbook of the National Society for the Study of Education, 106* (1), 186–216. Retrieved from http://onlinelibrary.wiley.com/doi/10.1111/j.1744-7984 .2007.00102.x/references.

George, J., & Cowan, J. 1999. *A Handbook of Techniques for Formative Evaluation. MAPPING the Student's Learning Experience.* New York: Routledge.

Gibbs, G., & Simpson, C. 2004. "Conditions Under Which Assessment Supports Students' Learning." *Learning and Teaching in Higher Education, 1.* Retrieved from www2 .glos.ac.uk/offload/tli/lets/lathe/issue1/issue1.pdf#page=5.

Gottlieb, M., Cranley, M. E., & Oliver, A. R. 2007. *WIDA English Language Proficiency Standards and Resource Guide, 2007 Edition, Pre-Kindergarten Through Grade 12.* Madison, WI: Board of Regents of the University of Wisconsin System, on behalf of the WIDA Consortium. Retrieved from www.wida.us/standards/eld.aspx#2007.

Hattie J., & Jaeger, R. 1998. "Assessment and Classroom Learning: A Deductive Approach." *Assessment in Education: Principles, Policy & Practice, 5* (1), 111–122. Retrieved from www.tandfonline.com/doi/abs/10.1080/0969595980050107?journalCode=caie20#. UjHYuD-kDYc.

Heritage, M. 2007. "Formative Assessment: What Do Teachers Need to Know and Do?" *Phi Delta Kappan, 89* (2), 140–145.

Heritage, M. 2008. *Learning Progressions: Supporting Instruction and Formative Assessment.* Paper prepared for the Formative Assessment for Students and Teachers (FAST), State Collaborative on Assessment and Student Standards (SCASS) of the Council of Chief State School Officers (CCSSO), Washington, DC. Retrieved from www .ccsso.org/Documents/2008/Learning_Progressions_Supporting_2008.pdf.

Heritage, M. 2010a. *Formative Assessment: Making It Happen in the Classroom.* Thousand Oaks, CA: Corwin.

Heritage, M. 2010b. *Formative Assessment and Next-Generation Assessment Systems: Are We Losing an Opportunity?* Paper prepared for the Formative Assessment for Students and Teachers (FAST), State Collaborative on Assessment and Student Standards (SCASS) of the Council of Chief State School Officers (CCSSO), Washington, DC. Retrieved from http://www.edweek.org/media/formative_assessment_next _generation_heritage.pdf.

Heritage, M. 2013. *Formative Assessment in Practice: A Process of Inquiry and Action.* Cambridge, MA: Harvard Education Press.

Marzano, R. J. 2006. *Classroom Assessment & Grading That Works.* Alexandria, VA: Association for Supervision and Curriculum Development.

McKay, P. 2005. "Research into Assessment of School-Age Language Learners." *Annual Review of Applied Linguistics, 25,* 243–263.

McMillan, J. H. 2001. "Secondary Teachers' Classroom Assessment Grade Practices." *Educational Measurement Issues and Practices, 20* (1), 20–32.

McMillan, J. H. 2003. "Understanding and Improving Teachers' Classroom Assessment Decision Making: Implications for Theory and Practice." *Educational Measurement Issues and Practices, 22* (4), 5–12.

Michigan Department of Education. 2010. *Developing and Implementing the Formative Assessment Process in Michigan: A Guide for Classroom and Student Success.* Dover, NH: Measured Progress.

National Research Council. 2001. *Knowing What Students Know: The Science and Design of Educational Assessment.* Committee on the Foundations of Assessment. Pellegrino, J., Chudowsky, N., & Glaser, R. (Eds.), Board on Testing and Assessment, Center for Education, Division of Behavioral and Social Sciences and Education. Washington, DC: National Academies Press.

National Research Council. 2012. *Education for Life and Work: Developing Transferable Knowledge and Skills in the 21st Century.* Committee on Defining Deeper Learning and 21st Century Skills. Pellegrino, J., & Hilton, M. (Eds.), Center for Education, Board on Testing and Assessment, Division of Behavioral and Social Sciences and Education. Washington, DC: National Academies Press.

Nicol, D., & Macfarlane-Dick, D. 2006. "Formative Assessment and Self-Regulated Learning: A Model and Seven Principles of Good Feedback Practice." *Studies in Higher Education, 31*(2), 208.

No Child Left Behind Act of 2001 (NCLB). Pub. L. No. 107–110, §115, Stat. 1425. 2002. USA.

Popham, W. J. 1995. *Classroom Assessment: What Teachers Need to Know.* Needham Heights, MA: Allyn & Bacon.

Popham, W. J. 2008. *Transformative Assessment.* Alexandria, VA: Association for Supervision and Curriculum Development.

Redfield, D., Roeber, E., & Stiggins, R. 2008. *Building Balanced Assessment Systems to Guide Educational Improvement.* Background paper for the keynote panel presentation at the National Conference on Student Assessment, Council of Chief State School Officers, Orlando, FL, June 2008. Retrieved from www.maine.gov/education/diploma/ccssobuildingassessment.pdf.

Ross, D. A. 2005. "Streamlining Assessment—How to Make Assessment More Efficient and More Effective—An Overview." In: Quality Assurance Agency for Higher Education (Ed.), *Reflections on Assessment: Volume I.* Gloucester, Scotland: Quality Assurance Agency for Higher Education, 12–14.

Shepherd, L. A. 2006. "Classroom Assessment." In: R. L. Brennen (Ed.), *Educational Measurement* (4th ed.). Westport, CT: Praeger.

Short, D. J., & Fitzsimmons, S. 2007. *Double the Work: Challenges and Solutions to Acquiring Language and Academic Literacy for Adolescent English Language Learners.* New York: Carnegie Corporation.

Shute, V. J. 2008. "Focus on Formative Feedback." *Review of Educational Research, 178* (1), 153–189.

Stiggins, R. J. 2001. "The Unfulfilled Promise of Classroom Assessment." *Educational Measurement Issues and Practices, 20* (3), 5–15.

Stiggins, R. J. 2005. "From Formative Assessment to Assessment FOR Learning: A Path to Success in Standards-Based Schools." *Phi Delta Kappan, 87* (4), 324–328.

Tuttle, H. G. 2009. *Successful Student Writing Through Formative Assessment.* Larchmont, NY: Eye on Education.

Vygotksy, L. 1986. *Thought and Language.* Cambridge, MA: The MIT Press.

Wiliam, D. 2012. *Embedded Formative Assessment.* Bloomington, IN: Solution Tree Press.

Zwiers, J. 2008. *Building Academic Language: Essential Practices for Content Classrooms.* San Francisco, CA: Jossey-Bass.

INDEX

A

Academic English. *See* Academic language

Academic language
  development of, xiv–xv, 75–77
  in instruction, 2–5, 9
  perspectives of, 72
  student involvement, 3–4
  teacher background in, 2
Argument genre, 5–6, 11–14, 33, 49, 64
Assessment. *See* Formative assessment; Self feedback

B

Bailey, Alison, 70
Balanced language assessment system, xv–xvii, 70–71
Bransford, J.D., xiv
Brown, A.L., xiv

C

Checklist for self feedback, 56–60, 64–65, 72
Cocking, R.R., xiv
Collocations, 35
Constitutional Convention lesson, 11–12, 31–33
Criteria, for success. *see* Success criteria

D

Data collection. *See* Formative assessment
Data collection tools, 56–60, 64–65, 72
Davis, Kevin, xxii, 11–13, 48, 55–56
Derewianka, B., 5
Dynamic Language Learning Progression, xiii, 19

E

EngineSim, 14
Erickson, Fred, 55

F

FAME (Formative Assessment for Michigan Educators), 72
Feedback. *See also* Self feedback
  designing, 2–5
  formative language defined, xiv–xvii, 41–42
  to Jorge, 44–47, 52, 60–63
  to Kia, 47–50, 64–65
  to Migdalia, 16–17, 38–39, 50–52, 66–68
  peer, 42–43, 60–61
  tools for, 56–60, 72
FLARE (Formative Language Assessment Records for English Language Learners), xiii, 18–19, 56, 75–77
Formative assessment. *See also* Self feedback
  analysis of writing for, 18, 26–35
  characteristics of, 41–42
  data collection tools for, 56–60, 64–65, 72
  grades in, 72
  history of, xii–xiii
  IDEAL Model, xix–xxi
  language opportunities, 17
  lesson-embedded, 55–56
  rating scales for, 58–61
  rubrics for, 58–60, 66–67
  sources of, 42–43
  stages of, xviii–xix
  student involvement in, 41, 43
  use of, 5
  views on, 41

Formative Assessment for Michigan
Educators (FAME), 72
Formative Language Assessment Records
for English Language Learners (FLARE),
xiii, 18–19, 56, 75–77
Formative language feedback, defined,
xiv–xvii

G

Gardner, Jason. *See also* Jorge; Kia;
Migdalia
data gathering tools, 56–60, 64–65,
72
introduction, xxii
student work analysis, 26–37
working with teachers, 8–17
Genre components
argument, 5–6, 11–14, 33, 49, 64
demonstration of, 5–6, 8–9
in Jorge's writing, 27–28, 46–47,
62–63
in Kia's writing, 32–33, 49, 64
in language analysis, 19–24
in Migdalia's writing, 39, 51, 53, 68
narrative/recount, 5–6
process/procedure, 5–10
report, 5–6
Grades, effect of, 72
Grammatical forms
in Jorge's writing, 28, 30, 47, 63
in Kia's writing, 32–34, 50, 65
language analysis of, 19–24
language learning targets, 25–26
in Migdalia's writing, 38–39, 53, 68
Reference Performance Level
Descriptors (RPLD), 3–4, 20–22

H

Heritage, Margaret, xi, 5, 40, 70
How People Learn (Bransford, Brown, and
Cocking), xiv

I

IDEAL Model, xix–xxi
Inquiry-based approach, 72

J

Jorge
feedback for, 44–47, 52, 60–63
genre components for, 27–28, 30,
46–47, 62–63
grammatical forms, 28, 30, 47, 63
introduction, xxii–xxiii
language assessment process, 10,
29–31, 45–47, 62–63
language learning targets, 26–29, 44–45
language sample analysis, 26–28, 29–31
procedure writing in math, 9–10
rating scales for, 60–61
self feedback tools for, 61–62
success criteria, 9, 30, 44–46, 62
text structure, 28, 30, 47, 63
vocabulary, 28, 61–62

K

Kia
feedback for, 47–50, 64–65
genre components for, 32–33, 49, 64
grammatical forms, 32–34, 50, 65
introduction, xxiii
language assessment process, 14,
33–34, 49–50, 64–66
language learning targets, 32–33, 48
language sample analysis, 31–34
self feedback tools for, 56–57, 64–65
success criteria, 14, 29, 33, 48–49,
64–65
text structure, 33, 49, 65
vocabulary, 12–14, 31–33, 72

L

Language. *See* Academic language
Language Analysis Lenses, 19–24

Language assessment process
    for Jorge, 11, 30–31, 45–47, 62–63
    for Kia, 14, 33–34, 49–50, 65–66
    for Migdalia, 16–17, 38–39, 52–54,
       66–68
Language learning progressions (LLP), 48,
   75–77
Language learning targets (LLT)
    design of, xviii–xx
    grammatical forms, 25–26
    for Jorge, 26–29, 44–45
    for Kia, 32–33, 48
    lenses for, 19–24
    for Migdalia, 35–37
    student samples, 26–37
    through success criteria, 25–26
Language sample analysis
    for Jorge, 26–28, 29–31
    for Kia, 31–34
    for Migdalia, 34–39
Learning progressions, 3–4

M
Math lesson, 7–10, 26–27, 30–31, 45–47,
   62–63, 75
Michigan Department of Education, 72
Migdalia
    feedback for, 16–17, 38–39, 50–52,
       66–68
    genre components for, 39, 51, 53, 68
    grammatical forms, 39, 53, 68
    introduction, xxiii
    language assessment process, 16–17,
       38–39, 52–54, 66–68
    language learning targets, 35–37
    language sample analysis, 34–35
    self feedback tools for, 66–67
    success criteria, 16–17, 34–35, 38,
       52, 67
    text structure, 38, 53, 68
    vocabulary, 66–67

N
Narrative/Recount genre, components in,
   5–6
National Research Council, 1
Next Generation Science Standard (NGSS),
   14
Nominalization, 37, 51–52, 67

P
Peer feedback, 42–43, 60–61
Performance Level Descriptors (PLDs), 18,
   34–35
Process/Procedure genre, 5–10
Professional development, 72

R
Race to the Top, 71
Rating scales, 58–61
Reference Performance Level Descriptors
   (RPLD), 3–4, 20–22
Register (writing), 15, 34–35, 35, 37, 50
Report genre, components in, 5–6
Rubrics, 58–60, 66–67

S
Santos, Elena. *See also* Jorge; Kia;
   Migdalia
    introduction, xxii
    procedure writing in math, 7–10
    student work analysis, 26–29
Scaffolding activities, 9, 15
Science lesson, 4–5, 14–17, 34–35, 38–39,
   52–53, 66–67, 75
Self feedback. *See also* Feedback;
   Formative assessment
    self-assessment, 4, 42–43, 52, 56
    self-monitoring, 56–57, 64–65
    self-reflection, 43
    tools for, 56–60, 72
Social studies lesson, 11–14, 33–34, 48–50,
   64–65, 75

Success criteria
  for Jorge, 10, 30, 44–46, 62
  for Kia, 14, 31, 33, 48–49, 64–65
  for Migdalia, 16–17, 34–35, 38, 52, 67
  through language learning targets
    (LLTs), 25–26
  through learning progressions, 3–4

T
Text structure
  defined, 22
  in Jorge's writing, 28, 31, 46, 63
  in Kia's writing, 33, 49, 65
  in language analysis, 24
  in Migdalia's writing, 38, 53, 68
Tools
  for formative assessment, 56–60, 72
  for Jorge language assessment, 61–62
  for Kia language assessment, 64
  for Migdalia language assessment,
    66–68

V
Vocabulary
  in Jorge's writing, 28, 61–62
  in Kia's writing, 12–14, 30–33, 72
  in language analysis, 19–24
  in Migdalia's writing, 39, 66–67
  from primary sources, 12–14
  usage, 22
Vygotsky, Lev, 18

W
"Write Like a Scientist Day," 15–16
Writing analysis, 18, 26–35. *See also* Jorge;
  Kia; Migdalia